Aurora Slot Cars

Thomas Graham

4880 Lower Valley Road · Atglen, PA 19310

Disclaimer

An earlier version of this book was published by Kalmbach Books in 1995 under the title *Greenberg's Guide to Aurora Slot Cars*. Photos and text are used with the permission of Kalmbach Books.

Aurora® and AFX are registered trademarks of Tomy Corporation. Model Motoring is a registered trademark of Model Motoring, Inc. The oval Aurora logo is a registered trademark of CineModels, Inc. ThunderJet 500 is a registered trademark of Playing Mantis, Inc. This book is neither authorized nor approved by any of the trademark holders and use of the Aurora, AFX, Model Motoring, ThunderJet 500 names is solely for identification purposes.

Library of Congress Control Number: 2003104233

Designed by Joseph M. Riggio Jr.
Type set in Americana Xbd BT/Dutch801 Rm BT

ISBN: 978-0-7643-1863-4
Printed in China
6 5 4 3

Published by Schiffer Publishing, Ltd.
4880 Lower Valley Road
Atglen, PA 19310
Phone: (610) 593-1777; Fax: (610) 593-2002
E-mail: Info@schifferbooks.com
Web: www.schifferbooks.com

Acknowledgments

Among the greatest pleasures derived from researching this book was meeting the people who love little electric cars—people who celebrate the romance of the slotted road. Many of these individuals know far more about this subject than I, and I freely acknowledge my debt to them. Among the most helpful sources of information were Bob Beers, Greg Holland, Jim Johnson, Dave Lockwood, Ron Esterline, Phil Frank, Mark Mattei, Scott Ronhock, Edward Sourbeck, Kevin Timothy, and Bill Wessels. Howard Kilgore read the manuscript.

Photographs of HO and 1/48 scale cars were taken in the home of Bob Beers, to whom I give enormous thanks. Dave Lockwood furnished his AFX cars for the photo shoot. Photos of the 1/32, 1/25, and 1/24 cars were taken by Gary Gerding. Among the cars in these photos are some loaned by Bernard Sampson and Emil Bertolini.

Detailed information on colors, model variations, and prices came from Bob "Mr. Aurora" Beers and Howard Johansen. Every serious slot car collector needs to purchase a copy of Bob's *Complete Color Guide to Aurora Slot Cars*, which is the ultimate authority on every detail of Aurora's Vibrators, Thunderjets, and AFXs.

Collectors who are interested in cars produced by Tomy under the Tomy AFX/Aurora name between the years 1986-1997 should find a copy of Robert Budano's *Complete Guide to Collecting Tomy H. O. Scale Slot Cars*.

The perspective from inside the Aurora plant was supplied by many individuals intimately connected with the company. I would first like to thank Marie Cuomo, Maria Shikes, Eleanor Giammarino, and Joseph Giammarino, who together with John Cuomo and Abe Shikes first agreed to the formation of Aurora over dinner in Brooklyn in 1950. Thanks also to Mr. Charles M. Diker, Aurora president in the 1970s.

The list of other former Aurora personnel and hobby industry leaders who helped me encompasses an awesome array of talent and experience: Robert Bernhard, Derek Brand, John E. Brodbeck, Frank Carver, Richard Cohen, Raymond Haines, Kenneth Hill, Homer Leovas, Jim Keeler, Jim Kirby, Michael Meyers, Walter Moe, Richard Palmer, Nat Polk, Richard Ratkiewich, Jim Russell, Richard Schwarzchild, Donald "Bill" Silverstein, and John Vernon. Former Aurora staffer Andrew P. Yanchus has published many articles about Aurora that were valuable in researching this book.

Thanks is also due the staff of the periodicals section of the Library of Congress, and to Maurice and David Gherman, who gave me access to the archives of *Craft, Model and Hobby Industry* Magazine.

My deepest thanks to all of the above—and to many others too numerous to mention—who shared their knowledge with me and often saved me from errors of fact and interpretation. Any mistakes that may have escaped their notice are my responsibility.

Preface

Aurora is a name from which legends have arisen. For nearly thirty years, Aurora Plastics Corporation led the way in popularizing some of the most spectacularly successful hobbies of the modern era, including plastic model kits and electric slot cars. Because Aurora created innovative and intriguing products, produced them well, and showed enterprise in marketing them, it rose by the 1960s to become the world's largest hobby company. In the 1970s Aurora expanded even further, becoming one of the nation's foremost producers of tabletop games. Then, in the tumultuous business climate of the 1970s, Aurora disappeared. The untimely demise only adds to their mystique.

Today Aurora's classic plastic model kits and slot cars are highly collectible. My goal in writing this book is to provide accurate information to collectors about Aurora slot cars manufactured between 1960 and 1977, the year of the original Aurora company's demise. I'll also explain the origins of slot cars, give an inside-the-factory look at how Aurora made its cars, and relate the story of how slot car racing became one of the most popular pastimes of the 1960s and 1970s.

Contents

Chapter One
Slot Cars: A Fast Start

Aurora Plastics Corporation received its charter from the state of New York on March 9, 1950 and began operations in August in a converted garage on 62nd Street in Brooklyn. At the beginning Aurora operated as a contract molding shop, making plastic products for a variety of customers, mostly in the novelty jewelry business. Soon it was plastic clothes hangers and toy bow and arrow sets for dime stores—very basic jobs for a small molding company with about a dozen employees.

Then in the fall of 1952, Aurora made a decided change of direction and introduced a line of inexpensive all-plastic model airplane kits. Not only were the kits among the first of their kind, but Aurora's products were marketed through chain stores.

Successful mass marketing by Aurora and other companies such as Revell brought modeling out of side street hobby shops and into Main Street variety stores. In large part because of these inexpensive Aurora kits, model building became the most popular hobby of 1950s American boys.

Aurora's founders: John Cuomo, Abe Shikes, and Joe Giammarino. *Rod & Custom Models.*

The Founding

Aurora owed its success to its founders Abe Shikes and Joseph Giammarino, who teamed-up to turn good ideas and hard work into an extremely profitable business enterprise.

Shikes was born in Russia in 1908 and immigrated to New York City in the 1920s, where he built his career manufacturing inexpensive jewelry. He proved to have a knack for finding what he called "good things"—products that would sell. Short in stature, emotional, and aggressive by nature, Shikes brought tough-minded leadership to Aurora. The chain-smoking, fast-talking Shikes operated as front man for the company.

Brooklyn native Giammarino was a perfect complement to Shikes. Silent and reserved, Joe found it easier to keep his temper under control while working with machines than when dealing with people. He came from a family of jewelry makers—and also happened to be a college-trained electrical engineer. At Aurora he supplied the creative spark to the manufacturing process and kept the wheels of production turning.

The pair founded Aurora with the financial backing of silent partners. The 1952 departure of those partners forced a reorganization of the company. Enter John Cuomo, the third major figure in Aurora's rise. Born in Italy in 1901, Cuomo came aboard as sales manager and junior partner. Personable and outgoing, Cuomo was Aurora's spokesman to advertisers, distributors, and retailers.

Brisk demand for Aurora plastic models caused the young company to quickly outgrow its makeshift Brooklyn facility. Aurora moved to a large, modern plant in December 1953. The location—44 Cherry Valley Road, West Hempstead, Long Island—would remain Aurora headquarters throughout the rest of the firm's history. Soon after relocation, Aurora initiated production of a hobbycraft line: Coppersmith kits for producing embossed copper plaques; Air Champ Radio, crystal radio kits; and by 1959, ready-to-fly model airplanes for department stores.

Model airplanes did well for Aurora. To assure a continuous supply of engines, Aurora in 1960 purchased K&B Allyn, a California manufacturer of gas-powered airplane motors. K&B had been founded by Ludwig Kading and

John E. Brodbeck in 1944, and one of its first products was a minor component for the A-bomb. When Aurora bought K&B in 1960, Brodbeck owned and managed the company. A genial person, well known in the hobby industry, Brodbeck was an expert designer of model airplane motors. Aurora moved K&B from Compton to Downey and sent Sheldon "Shellie" Ostrowe from West Hempstead to California to oversee operations, but Brodbeck remained in charge of production.

John E. Brodbeck

In 1960 Aurora introduced another hobby product—electric-powered slot cars—and a generation of American youngsters went crazy over them. Aurora and subsidiary K&B emerged as the dominant builders of top-quality slot cars in both the mass-market toy field and the more demanding hobbyist segment.

Perhaps most important, Aurora succeeded in slot cars where others failed because they spent time, energy, and money showing youngsters how to have fun with miniature racers. Slot cars catapulted Aurora to the top of the hobby world—far ahead of model kit rival Revell, and very far ahead of venerable toy manufacturers like Lionel. It was the product line that ultimately defined the West Hempstead manufacturer.

Origins of the Slot Car

The distant ancestors of Aurora's slot cars were 19th-century windup toy games with racing horses, bicycles, and eventually automobiles. Mechanized toys were among the most popular Industrial Revolution-era playthings; their lifelike animation made them a hit with affluent toy consumers and, later, those of the working class.

Ironically, the closest toy to Aurora's slot cars originated in electric trains—the segment that would ultimately suffer the most with the advent of slot cars. In 1912, the Lionel Corporation, already famous for its electric trains, introduced an electric car set featuring metal 1/24 scale Stutz Bearcats rolling around a steel roadway on rubber tires. They were powered by model train motors and received electric current from a standard railroad track rail recessed in a slot.

Lionel's cars were sold only through 1916 and today are regarded as scarce collectibles. Though not very successful at retail, the Lionel toys did have one lasting effect: they introduced the concept of toy electric cars to the public. The idea was so basic and solid that it continued to arise again and again, both in Europe and the United States. In 1929 a Kokomo, Indiana, firm marketed an electric car whose front bumper picked up voltage from an electrified fence running alongside the roadway. In 1935 Louis Marx marketed a windup set

Lionel 1912 car set. *B. Schwab photograph.*

with cars that operated on a figure-eight roadway. The following year Marx electrified the set. The concept of electric road racing endured, but still didn't capture the toy buying public's attention like electric trains.

Adult hobbyists invented the sport of "rail car" racing in the late 1930s, and it developed a following in Great Britain and the American Midwest during the 1950s. Hobbyists formed clubs and scratch built elaborately detailed wood, fiberglass, and metal cars. The first examples were powered by gasoline engines, tethered to a post, and set to race on a circular track—what became known as thimble-drome racing. Other enthusiasts clamped their cars to a fixed, raised rail and turned them loose to run. Soon the rail went electric, and motors were scavenged from model locomotives. For the first time, the speed of an individual car could be controlled by a rheostat.

However, rail racing was a hobby for adults who read *Popular Mechanics.* The skills, tools, and money needed to build the cars and the tracks were well beyond the average youngster. Noisy, smelly gasoline-powered cars had to stay outdoors, and rail cars—built in a variety of scales, but mostly 1/32—required garage or basement-sized space for an adequate layout.

British Forebears

It was only a matter of time until the hobby industry would see the intrinsic entertainment of miniature auto racing and respond with a commercial product that the average boy could play with in his home. The first company to do so was Scalextric of Great Britain. Frederick Francis introduced a home race set in 1956 and immediately the cars caught on in the European market. His metal Ferrari and Maserati Formula I race cars rolled on plastic wheels and were touted as capable of scale speeds up to 130 miles per hour. They were built to 1/30 scale to accommodate the rather bulky electric motors available at the time.

The success of Scalextric attracted the attention of the Polk brothers, Irwin and Nathan, of New York City. Widely regarded as the godfathers of the American hobby industry, the Polks ran an elaborate five-story hobby shop in Manhattan (which appears in the Christmas shopping scene in the *Godfather* movie). They marketed both imported products and their own line under the Aristo-Craft label. The Polks had been fiddling with the idea of developing their own pre-packaged rail car sets since the 1930s, but they liked Scalextric's commercial home racing set so much that they adopted it and became the American distributors.

The Polks introduced Scalextric at the Hobby Industry Association of America show in Chicago in 1957, but to their dismay only two American distributors placed orders, and over the next two years sales in the American market were equally barren. The reason: shipping costs from Europe raised the price tag to a hefty $50. In addition, Scalextric's conventional figure-eight layout just didn't excite the imagination. However, in Europe

Derek Brand in Aurora's bare-bones research and development shop. *Rod & Custom Models.*

sales of Scalextric's large-scale cars grew to be quite respectable, and Europeans permanently accepted 1/32 scale as the appropriate size for slot cars.

While Scalextric was putting large-scale slot cars on the road to success, development of a small-scale system came from a totally independent source.

The Father of HO Slot Cars

Credit for development of the HO slot car goes to Derek Brand, but he also was the originator of several other revolutionary products in the hobby and toy industries.

Born in England in 1926, Brand emigrated to the United States in 1948 and went to work for California company Gowland & Gowland, a toy industry design house owned by British expatriates Jack and Kelvin Gowland.

Short, balding, and cheery, Brand was a consummate, although self-taught, engineer and sculptor. In one of his assignments for Gowland, Brand helped develop a product that revolutionized the plastic model kit industry—Highway Pioneers plastic car model kits. Brand sculpted the body prototypes, called "patterns," from wood, which a tooling shop used to create the metal production dies central to the newly dominant toy making process of injection molding. Gowland leased marketing rights for Highway Pioneers to Revell, Inc. of Los Angeles, and Revell sold them as inexpensive hobby items through dime stores. When Aurora's model airplane kits hit the market shortly after Revell's cars, plastic models quickly zoomed in popularity and became one of the first fads of the 1950s.

In 1953 Jack Gowland relocated his company to Puerto Rico to take advantage of tax incentives offered by the US government to encourage industry there, and Brand went with him. Brand had already been tinkering with the concept of an electric home racing set, but now got down to some serious research. His first experiments involved putting Pittman model train motors inside metal die-cast Dinky cars. Brand supplied the cars with electric current through two strips of metallic paint sprayed onto the roadbed. The results were unsatisfactory: the motors were too big and too expensive, and the painted-powerstrip idea just didn't work.

Meanwhile, wanderlust caused Jack Gowland to move to Canada. He sold his company to businessman Carl Robinette, who proceeded to move everything back to California, settling in Santa Barbara in 1955. One

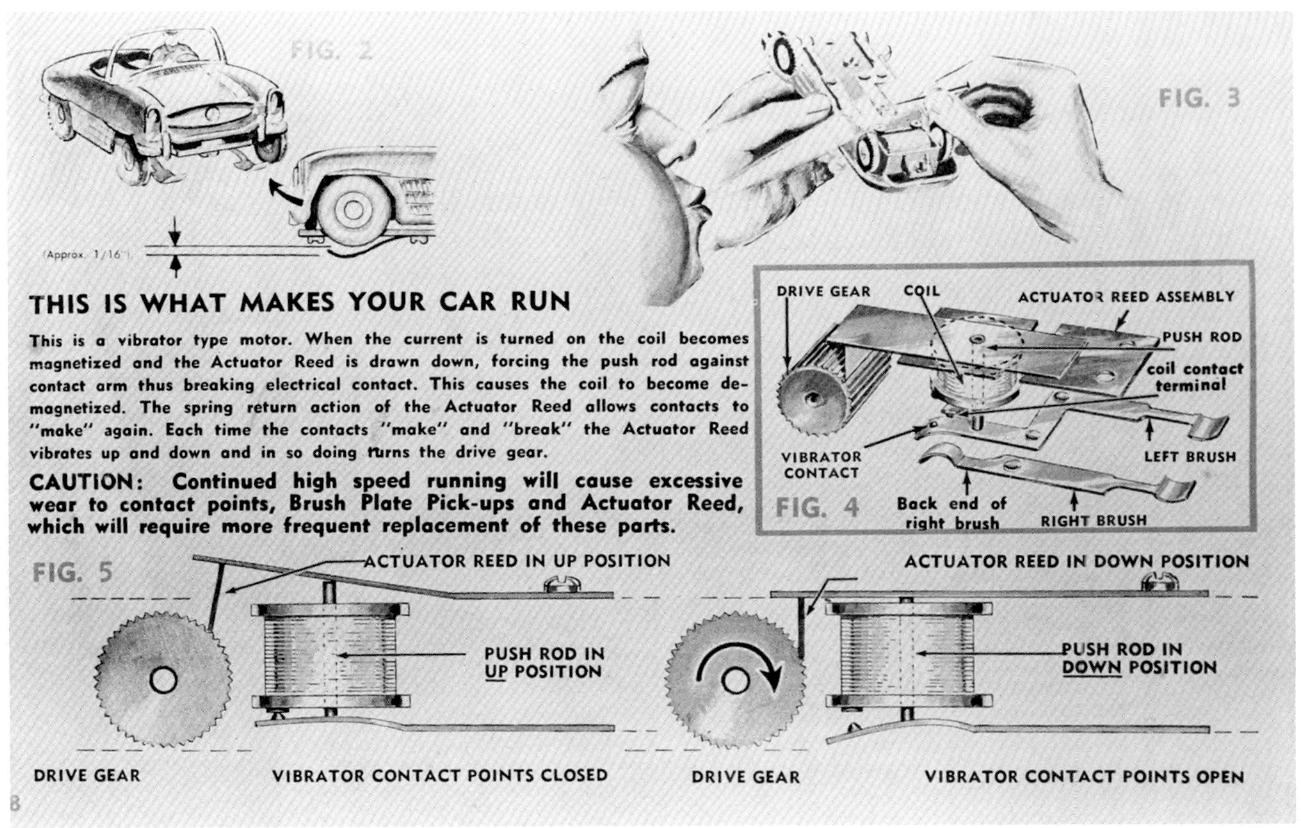

Derek Brand's ingenious vibrator motor design.

of Robinette's spinoff corporations was Crafco, where Brand was reassigned. Brand continued tweaking his electric car system. Brand conceived of his design as an accessory to HO model railroading and thus designed it in 1/87 to ensure compatibility with the newly popular model railroading scale. He wanted cars and trucks that could be steered around streets, over bridges, and through tunnels—like electric trains.

Brand totally ignored Scalextric's pioneering slot car work and developed his own system from the ground up. His first important breakthrough came when he finally solved the problem of supplying miniature cars with electricity. He abandoned the long-established configuration of an electrified central rail and, instead, went with the concept of two metal power strips offset on either side of the center slot. He figured out how to manufacture the metal strips by rolling a coil of wire flat and then chopping it into segments that could be embedding into the plastic road surface. With the track problem licked, only one challenge remained—creating the cars.

Birth of the Vibrator

Brand finally mastered the dilemma of getting bulky, expensive motors into very small car bodies simply by abandoning conventional motors. Brand designed his own motor using the concept of a common door buzzer—the "vibrator" motor. It was small enough to fit in a chassis less than 2" long. Brand had gotten little encouragement from Jack Gowland, who declared, "You'll never make a door buzzer run around a track!" But the determined Anglo-Californian did just that.

Brand's motor is a model of simplicity. An upright coil of wire becomes an electromagnet when electricity flows through it. The design places a flat metal actuator reed across the top of the coil. When the coil is magnetized by electricity, the actuator reed pulls toward the coil and ratchets a drive gear mounted on the car's rear axle. At the same time, the reed also forces down a rod passing through the coil. The downward motion of the rod pushes the rear end of the electrical pickup shoe away from the bottom of the coil, momentarily breaking electrical contact and demagnetizing the coil.

The actuator reed then springs back up and (at the bottom of the coil) the metal contact shoe does the same thing, reestablishing contact with the coil. This sends current through the coil once again, and the whole process starts anew. With 16 volts of alternating current flowing through the system, the process is repeated many times per second, sending the car literally buzzing down the track.

Highways: The First HO Slot Car Set

Carl Robinette knew he had a winner with Derek Brand's ingenious miniaturized car system. He began shopping the concept around to numerous toy companies, finally cutting a deal with British toy maker Mettoy, builder of Corgi die-cast cars. Low British tooling and production costs helped underwrite the launch of a speculative new product. Robinette retained ownership of the tooling, leasing it to Mettoy.

With great fanfare, Mettoy's Playcraft division unveiled Highways Road Transport System at the 1959 Brighton Toy Fair. Unfortunately, most English toy and hobby distributors were unimpressed. Highways arrived on the scene shortly after Scalextric, and it never achieved popularity in Great Britain (dying a natural death after only a few years).

During the fair, glum Playcraft marketers received a visit from Abe Shikes and Joe Giammarino of the United States. Since Playcraft distributed Aurora plastic model kits in Great Britain, Shikes and Giammarino were expected.

Shikes later relished telling the story of his discovery of slot cars. He recalled that one of the Playcraft representatives took him over to the booth. "We've got an item," he explained. Shikes was escorted to a small roadway layout with little two-inch cars resting on it. "He turns it on and I couldn't believe something so small could have a motor inside. I picked one up and put it down in a hurry—it was hot. Whenever anybody would come in to watch the cars, this guy would wet his fingers and pick up a car. I thought he was just picking them up, but what he was actually doing was cooling them off."

The two Americans surveyed the miniature car system and were surprised and delighted. Shikes and Giammarino discovered Derek Brand lurking behind a curtain, like the Wizard of Oz, operating the controls of his slot car layout.

Playcraft had just twelve hand-built prototype cars specially created by Brand. Only four would later go into production: the Jaguar XK140, Mercedes 300SL, Ford Lorry, and to please the anticipated American market, 1958 Chevrolet Impala (nos. 3101 through 3104). The speed controllers were green-painted metal with working "ignition" keys and tiny steering wheels operating the rheostats. Brand's vibrator motors could endure 150 to 200 hours of operation without breakdown. Previously he'd run numerous home tests, setting up a Highways system on his dining room table and letting cars run while he watched television. Interference on his TV screen assured Brand that his tiny motors were still humming away.

Playcraft's Highways. Note the rare Chevy Impala (3103 $700) at left, as well as the Jaguar XK-140 (3101 $175), Mercedes 300SL (3102 $150), and Ford Lorry (3104 $375). The tube on the bed of the Lorry kept the truck from rattling-around in its sales box.

Although Robinette had taken his slot car concept to Great Britain first, he always intended to market his product in the United States. However, when Shikes and Giammarino asked Robinette for an American license, he refused, saying Aurora wasn't large enough to handle the anticipated high volume.

Robinette returned to the U.S. after Brighton and tried to sell Highways to a number of big American toy manufacturers (including Mattel and A. C. Gilbert) but found no takers. Only then—and only after much persuasion by Shikes—did Robinette agree to license his car system to Aurora.

Al Davis, then a hobby dealer in international trade and later a vice president at Aurora, observed: "The guys who ran Aurora were real businessmen. They didn't pussyfoot around. They had the guts to do what others wouldn't do."

However, Shikes put the decision in a different perspective: "Let me tell you something. I was scared stiff. We had to guarantee them a half-million dollars a year for five years! We were still a young company. We were growing, but to guarantee that amount of money for five years. If we didn't make it..."

Launching HO in the States

Aurora introduced Highways to the American hobby industry in January 1960 at the Hobby Industry Association of America show in Chicago. Aurora's suite provided prime display space for two basic layouts: one, a simple oval; the other integrated into an HO train layout to demonstrate compatibility. To the delight of the Aurora men, Hobby shop distributors and big chain-store buyers loved it at first sight! Moreover, the children of industry leaders went crazy over it—however, not exactly as Shikes and Giammarino had intended. Kids raced the oval-track cars so fast they spun out. The HO train system intrigued the youngsters only because of its potential for car-train smash-ups.

When HIAA ended, Sylvan Sidney, editor of the trade journal *Craft, Model and Hobby Industry*, wrote, "I may be wrong, but the most exciting new product displayed at the Chicago show was Aurora's 'Highways,' an HO scale highway system that can be used in conjunction with HO trains, or used as a 'Highway' race track." Aurora took out a full page ad in the March 1960 toy industry journal *Playthings*: "An unbelievable new product destined to take its place among the best-selling items of all time!"—a claim that proved prophetic.

Back in West Hempstead, frenzied activity filled Aurora executive offices. The first issue to be resolved was the question of how the product would be marketed. Robinette and some Aurora staff thought it best to emphasize the HO automobiles as an add-on to model train layouts since HO scale railroading was one of the hottest segments in hobbies at the time.

Aurora's hyperactive advertising manager Donald "Bill" Silverstein led the faction that wanted to pitch slot cars as racers. Silverstein was a local Brooklyn boy who had grown up to play minor league professional

The first vibrators: Jaguar XK140 convertible (1541 $35), Mercedes-Benz 300SL convertible (1542 $65), Chevrolet Corvette convertible (1543 $100), Ford Thunderbird hardtop (1544 $85), Jag XK140 coupe (1545 $85) and Mercedes 300SL coupe (1546 $75), Corvette coupe (1547 $300), Ford Galaxie Sunliner (1548 $90), including factory-built motorless floor toy), and Galaxie 500 hardtop (1549 $65).

baseball, and then flew in World War II as a B-17 radio operator. He carried a scar on his forehead from the day a ME-109 shot down his plane and put him into a German POW camp. Thereafter Silverstein refused to fly in airplanes, but he was fanatical about fast cars and competitive sports.

"Kids love racing cars," declared Silverstein. With Giammarino's backing, Silverstein won the HO trains vs. race car debate. As a compromise, advertising and packaging would highlight racing scenes, but with an insert depicting the HO railroading tie-in. Silverstein prevailed on another point, as well; the "Highways" label was dropped as inappropriate for a racing set. Playcraft had used the full title "Electric Highways Model Motoring" on its sets, and Aurora decided to shorten it to just "Model Motoring."

Tooling Up

Aurora's next hurdle was production. The items displayed at HIAA were either borrowed from Playcraft or hand-built prototypes. Aurora had taken orders for tens of thousands of sets and promised September delivery, but had yet to produce their first car or section of track. And the clock was ticking.

Crafco's leased tooling was immediately shipped from Mettoy to the United States, but was declared unsuitable by Aurora's perfectionist chief engineer Joe Giammarino. Aurora production chief Frank Carver remembers being called into Giammarino's office and told that Aurora would have to cut its own tooling, as well as set up the whole manufacturing and assembly apparatus. "We'll give it a shot," replied the overwhelmed Carver.

The Ford '62 Galaxie hardtop (1549 $65) and '62 Galaxie Sunliner (1548 $90) cross in front of the hand-sculpted prototype of the Judges Stand (1451 $45).

The Aurora workday stretched from 7 a.m. to 10 p.m. and into the weekend. Joe Giammarino labored around the clock, taking catnaps in his office and living on black coffee. He remembered it as "quite a push." Aurora chief machinist Victor Kowalski re-engineered the Crafco die-cast chassis tool. His design was so good that Aurora's version was exported to Great Britain for use by Playcraft, which explains why period examples of Playcraft cars are found today with two chassis variations.

Aurora cut body tools with four cavities to quadruple production. Giammarino and Carver set up the assembly line; thirty Aurora workers—all women—were trained to bring slot car components together seamlessly. Derek Brand was pressed into service to show the ladies the finer elements of soldering techniques. Near the end of the line assembled cars were placed on electrified track and zipped to final packaging. The West Hempstead firm's Herculean effort paid off; by September Aurora began shipping the first of what would become 100,000 sets to department stores and hobby distributors. It was the beginning of something very big.

Television: Aurora's Best Friend

Slot cars were still an entirely new concept to mainstream American toy consumers. Model trains—yes. Mechanical cars—of course. But electric cars racing around plastic roadways?

This launch-era store banner suggests either a model railroad tie-in or table-top racing.

The box art for this early race set was done by Mort Kunstler, who later became famous as a painter of Civil War scenes.

To build consumer awareness for the new Aurora product line, Silverstein initiated advertising campaigns in popular national magazines. His reason for magazines: adult buyers would see Aurora's promotional efforts and respond at Christmas with racing sets for their children. A full-page piece in the November 3 *New York Times* said it all: "The Most Exciting New Hobby Sport Since Electric Trains."

Carl Robinette had been right about one thing—Aurora couldn't afford TV advertising. In fact, Aurora traditionally had one of the lowest advertising budgets in the hobby industry. In any case, ad man Silverstein was skeptical of Saturday morning kids' show advertising. He saw it as an expensive quagmire that might not bring the sales results Aurora wanted.

Still, Silverstein appreciated the value of television exposure and set out to charm free time out of the networks. He knew Dave Garroway was an avid car buff; so Silverstein managed to wrangle an invitation to appear on Garroway's NBC *Today Show*.

They matched skills in a televised ten-lap, figure-eight race, which Garroway won. Two days later the newly confirmed slot car enthusiast devoted ten minutes on Today to races between himself and world-class Grand Prix racers Sterling Moss, Oliver Gendenbien, and Joakim Bonnier. Later that month Silverstein raced Jack Parr and Hugh Downs on *The Tonight Show*. On a subsequent visit with Parr, Silverstein created a forty slot car traffic jam as a humorous tribute to New York traffic.

Perhaps most significant was the fact that each of these programs targeted adult viewers. Silverstein knew Aurora's relatively high priced sets would be purchased by adults, and his entire market program—print, television, and public events—focused on this most important demographic group. Ensnare the parents, went Aurora's logic, and purchase price would not be a problem.

Product Launch—Sort Of

Aurora introduced Model Motoring in the fall of 1960 with four sets: the 1502 set at $16.95, the 1503 set at $24.95; and two uncataloged sets, one of which sold for only $10.95. Aurora production chief Frank Carver: "It hit the market and went right off the shelves. Nobody had ever seen anything like it before." Hobby-shop consumers fought over sets and telephoned stores thirty miles away to reserve a set. Bill Silverstein declared, "It was the biggest Christmas gift at the time."

Slot cars, of course, were an entirely new product, and many buyers had little idea what they were purchasing. December 26, 1960, brought that point home for Aurora—it was a day of complete pandemonium at the West Hempstead factory. Silverstein recalled there was a "tremendous" line of people outside the front doors clamoring to get in. Their cry: "This darn car won't run! Will you please sell me two more?"

Aurora staff immediately set up a "repair shop" in the lobby to show people how to make the vibrator cars work. Joanna Cuomo (daughter of Aurora's sales manager) and Frank Carver's daughter Jane ran the repair tables. The scene was repeated at Polk's Manhattan store and in hobby shops across the land; people had trouble making the slot cars run, but they loved them anyway—and they wanted to buy more. Experiencing this level of immediate devotion wasn't lost on Aurora management. "We realized we had something tremendous," said Carver.

Part of the success was novelty—the cars were completely new to American toy consumers. However, imaginative packaging and promotion also contributed to the initial groundswell. In February and March of 1961, Kellogg's Corn Flakes boxes carried the Aurora Model Motoring logo on the front and rules for a contest to win free race sets on back. Millions of kids across America learned of Aurora Model Motoring at the breakfast table.

Even Kellogg's helped Model Motoring get off to a good start.

Aurora soon learned that the real profit from their fledgling product line would come not only with the initial set purchase but also with follow-up sales of separate-sale cars, add-on track items, and racing accessories. Though there was the expected rush of imitators soon after Model Motoring's launch, Aurora's competitors simply didn't have the variety the West Hempstead manufacturer offered. Aurora was far out in front and pulling away quickly.

Challenges

Success was tempered by reality. Aurora struggled with Model Motoring's biggest drawback, the vibrator motor. Although it probably could achieve its advertised top speed of 150 scale miles per hour, the vibrator motor was a temperamental little machine. Indeed, factory tests had revealed many opportunities for things to go wrong. Any dust on the track or dirt or carbonizing on contact points short-circuited the system. Ray Haines, chief of plastic kit development, discovered this problem when he took an Aurora factory race display to a Lime Rock, Connecticut, sports car rally. The cars worked fine until the real cars started racing. Dust kicked up and the Aurora slot cars shut down.

The source of the problem: the vibrator motor's actuator reed had to be adjusted just right. The first time an excited kid grabbed a car off the track, the reed or pickup shoes would bend and cause a malfunction. And with the excitement of slot car racing, this was a problem that was more than just common.

As a man whose job involved making lemonade from lemons, Bill Silverstein began turning this negative into a positive. He promoted the vibrator motor as something to be souped-up, just like the real thing. Privately he confessed, "You had to tinker with it or the bloody thing wouldn't work." Of course, all the other manufacturers jumping into the slot car business had similar problems—only their dilemmas were often worse.

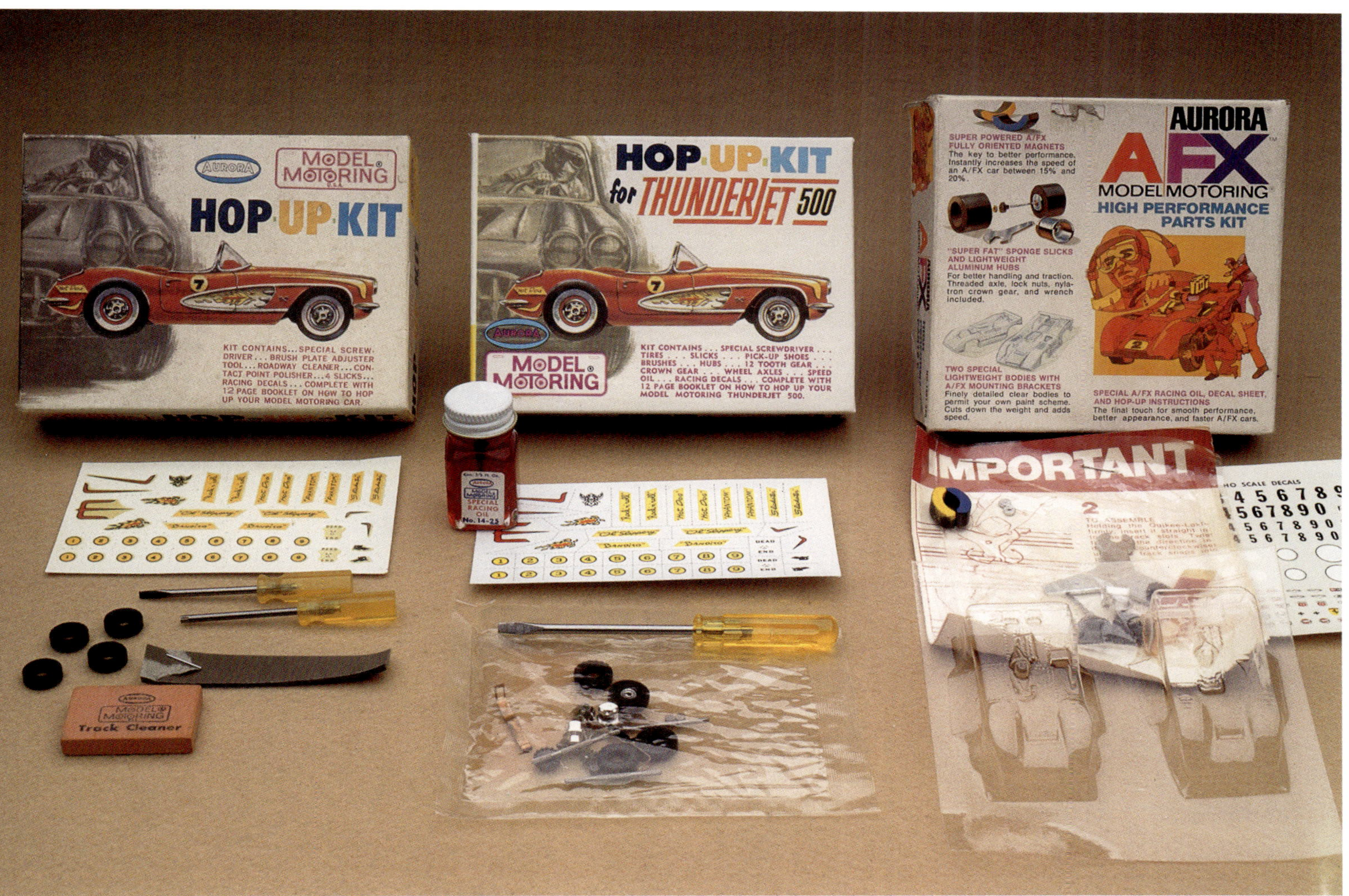

The Vibrator Hop-Up Kit included sandpaper for cleaning contact points and a slotted pick-up shoe adjustor. The Thunderjet edition added a jar of racing oil and some spare parts, while the AFX issue added vacuum-formed clear bodies.

The original design prototype for the Pit Kit carrying case.

The idea for a partial solution came from Rich Palmer and Dick Schwarzchild of R & R Analysis, a hobby industry consulting firm. Schwarzchild operated a Kingston, Pennsylvania, hobby shop and had experienced the flood of returns after Christmas 1960. A blunt-spoken man, Schwarzchild considered the vibrator car "a terrible product." Palmer ran Rich's Hobbytowne and Tri-O-Rama Field in Parsippany, New Jersey. Rich had also sold out Aurora slot sets, but experienced fifty percent returns after the holiday selling season.

To handle the returns, Palmer set up a repair shop and staffed it with local kids. "Adults would come in and say 'I can't make this work.' So a ten-year-old would open it up, and two seconds later away it would go." Palmer noted how the boys fiddled with the cars. From these observations he and Schwarzchild envisioned the "Hop Up Kit," a slot car accessory filled with tools, additional equipment, and a booklet of helpful hints.

They took the idea to Joe Giammarino and Derek Brand, who was dividing his time between California and West Hempstead. The four men worked out the details. Palmer wanted to include a pick-up shoe adjuster—a small screwdriver with the end sawed off and a slot cut in the end. (Lionel sold a similar tool for working on locomotive motors.) Joe Giammarino argued against the tool, citing cost and the fact that bends in the pick-ups and reed could be made without it.

Palmer won, and the adjusting tool went into the Hop Up Kit. Also included was a screwdriver, strips of fine sandpaper for cleaning the coil contact point, four oversized tires, track cleaner (an eraser), decal sheet, and "Hop-Up Hints" booklet. The Hop Up Kit sold for ninety-eight cents and instantly became one of Aurora's most popular products; equally important, it bought Aurora precious development time in the pursuit of a new motor design for its growing slot car product line.

Always Stylish, Always Contemporary

From the beginning of its involvement in slot cars, Aurora devoted plenty of attention to Model Motoring body styles. Aurora management believed that a wide variety would promote sets and subsequent car sales. At a time when other companies could offer only two to four body styles, Aurora introduced one new car after another. By 1962—barely two years after launch—there were nineteen cars and trucks in the Model Motoring line. Competitors simply could not match Aurora's pace.

Aurora inherited the first two Model Motoring cars from Playcraft: the 1541 Jaguar and 1542 Mercedes. The Chevrolet Impala was not continued because its body had too many parts for easy assembly and because the

The Ford Country Squire Wagon (1550 $55), Ford F-100 Pickup (1551 $75), Ford Galaxie Police Car (1552 $100), Hot Rod (1553 roadster $80, 1554 coupe $20), International Semi Tractor (1580 $120), pulling Van Body Trailer (1585 $120) and Box-Body Trailer (1584 $25), Mack Dump Truck (1582 $95), and 6-Wheel Mack Stake Truck (1583 $125).

'58 Chevy had quickly gone out of style. To enhance the American appeal of Model Motoring, Aurora added a Chevrolet Corvette convertible (1543) and Ford Thunderbird (1544)—the first models to be designed entirely in-house.

Interestingly, the plastic used in the vibrator cars wasn't regular styrene but rather cycolac (ABS), a substance that could withstand the heat generated by the motor. Cycolac is the same material used in period telephone casings, so early Model Motoring cars often resemble phone colors of the day. This explains Aurora's turquoise cars; it was a popular early-1960s hue for kitchen phones. Black, of course, was available, but Aurora made few in this color because they didn't show up well against black track.

Model Motoring sets came with a power controller (1533) similar to the original Playcraft version. The main changes were color and composition (from green-painted metal to gray ABS) and elimination of the ignition key. Like the cars, the controllers heated up. The tiny steering wheel speed control enhanced the illusion that you were driving a car, but in the excitement of a race the wheel tended to snap off—a definite party-ender for kids.

Aurora's sales department loved the clear plastic boxes that held Aurora's products, but most boys didn't care about the packaging. The Hot Rod roadster (1553 $75) and Mack Dump Truck (1582 $95).

This in-store banner shows that Aurora didn't know just how kids might play with their new slot cars.

The Crisscross track section with a McLaren Elva (1397 $35) leading a Dune Buggy Roadster (1398 $40).

The runaway success of Model Motoring created a monstrous demand for roadway track. Aurora manufactured sections by the millions, and feeding the molding machines with raw plastic became a major problem. As a short-term solution, Aurora jobbed out a substantial portion of track production to New York-area molding shops. But still the matter of sourcing enough material remained. Because of Aurora's huge appetite for plastic, Abe Shikes negotiated with suppliers across the country for inexpensive materials. His solution: combine recycled plastic—which Carver deemed "garbage"—with fresh raw plastic, color everything black, and start the machines. Joe Giammarino constantly objected to the low-grade material, arguing that quality be maintained. Out of their debate emerged "track black," an industry wide standard for roadway-grade plastic.

In the early years Aurora track was difficult to assemble. The instruction sheet even depicted three hands putting the track together! If two track sections didn't make contact perfectly, the electric power would not flow and a frustrated kid had to disassemble the whole track to locate the problem. Still, Aurora's selection of track sections was unparalleled in the toy industry. Perhaps most useful was the "crisscross," which alternated cars between lanes, eliminating the need for a figure eight and overpass to make lane distance equal between the two competing cars. This kind of simple innovation kept Aurora sets well ahead of the competition.

A Mack Stake Truck (1583 $70) on the R. R. Crossing.

The Train Tie-in

Although Aurora marketed slot cars primarily as racers, the company retained interest in the model railroad market. The first Model Motoring instruction manuals suggested a model railroading tie-in: "If you've already got an HO railroad system, Model Motoring in HO scale can be worked into it without any trouble at all. Just imagine how great it will be to have real cars and trucks barreling down real roads!" The railroad crossing section (1522) made it possible to fully integrate car and train systems.

Parkway Industries of Cleveland, Ohio, took the concept one step further. They packaged Aurora slot cars and Tyco trains together in a "Race-Road-Rail" set, available from 1961 to 1963. The set retailed for $60—a steep price for a hybrid product—and included Aurora Thunderbird and Corvette cars along with a Tyco Santa Fe diesel and three cars. The potential for train-auto wrecks was highlighted in ads—certainly not the ultimate in decorum, but definitely a tip of the hat to what children would be doing with their Race-Road-Rail sets.

Aurora had been making plastic model house kits for HO railroading since the late 1950s. Offering structures appropriate to scale auto racing seemed natural, beginning with the 658 Service Station, a Texaco gas station complete with a billboard proclaiming it a "Model Motoring Service Center." However, once it became clear model railroaders were interested in trains, not cars, Aurora discontinued the Service Station.

Aurora moved from producing structure kits for model railroading landscapes to making them for slot car layouts.

However, structure kits for slot cars was still a valid concept—Aurora simply needed better inspiration. In 1963 it announced nine new Model Motoring kits, including six that were never issued: first aid building, maintenance building, hay bales and hedges, billboard and signs, hot dog stand, and trophy presentation platform. Of the five kits produced, the Start-Finish Pylons (1450) seems to have been least popular. The Double Station Pit Stop (1453) was continually in demand, since kids considered it a good spot to park their extra cars. The Curved Bleachers (1456) fit the outside radius of Aurora's curved track perfectly. Kids across America spent their savings on these add-ons, boosting Aurora's profits.

The Gas Station (658 $150) is by far the toughest structure kit for collectors to find today.

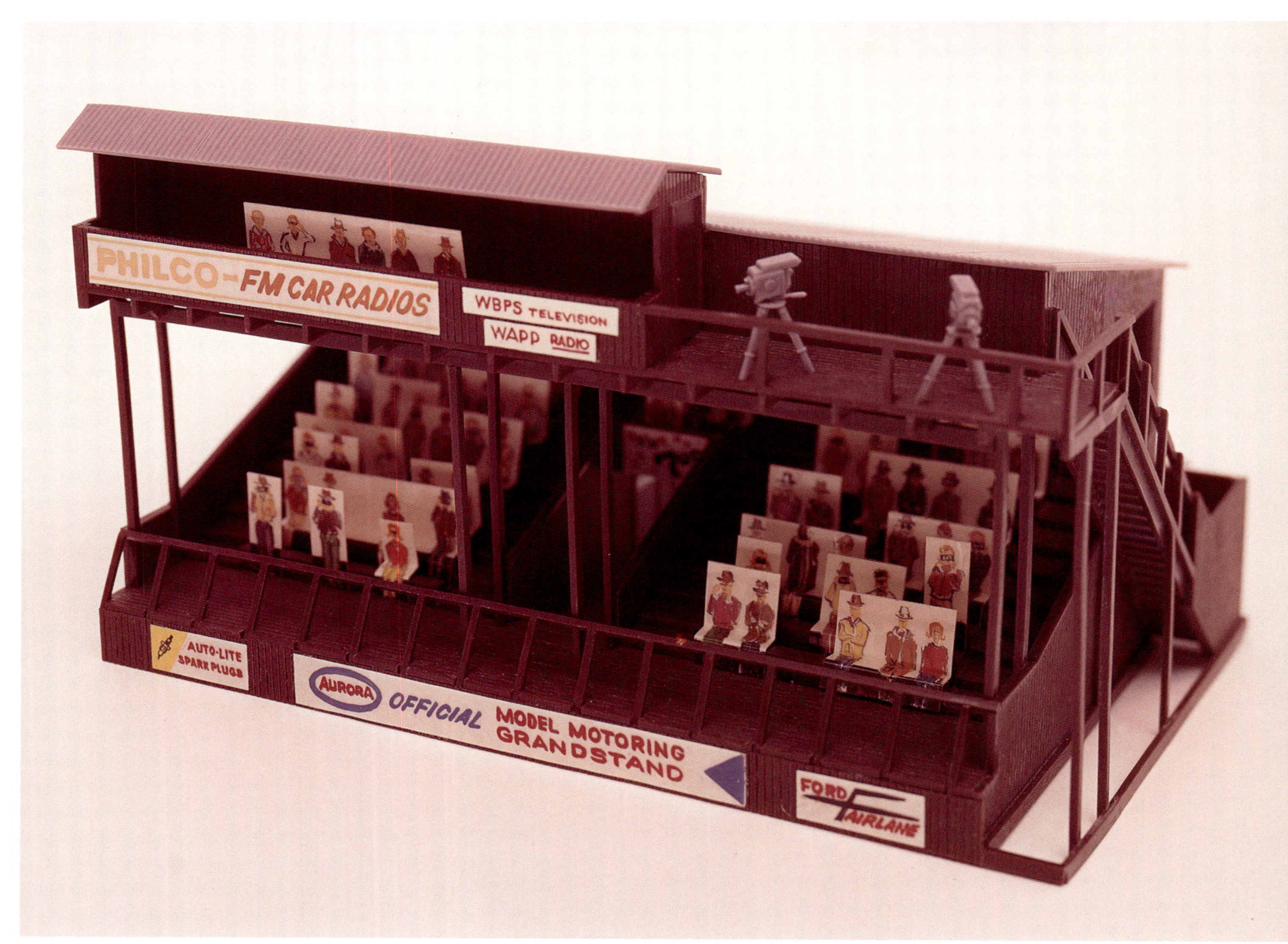

The original hand-made pattern for the Grandstand (1452 $45).

The Double Station Pit Stop (1453 $60) gave kids a place to park their extra cars.

The Pit Palace never made it to stores or the Model Motoring landscape.

The Grand National

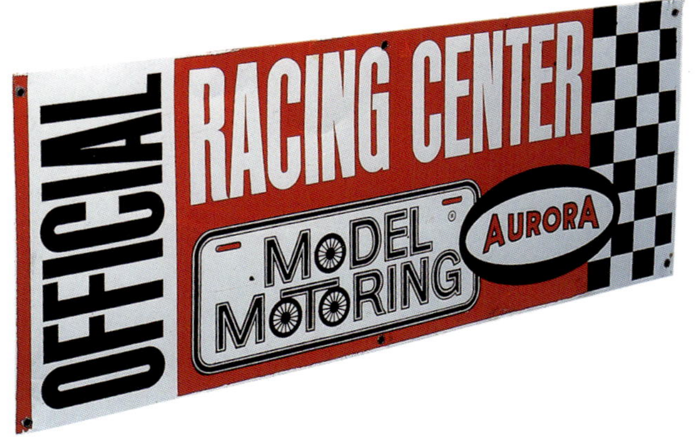

A rare pre-Thunderjets store "racing center" tin sign.

Rich Palmer's Tri-O-Rama Field did a larger volume of business than any hobby shop in America. One reason for his success over the years was his enterprise in organizing promotional contests to bring hobbyists into the store. People had flocked in to race thimble-drome cars, rail cars, Scalextric cars, and even Lionel trains. In the summer of 1961 he conducted six weekly races featuring Aurora slot cars exclusively. As part of his routine, he sent a newsletter to Aurora headquarters to report on his activities.

Silverstein paged through Palmer's newsletters one day and caught the mention of the Aurora races. He sent his assistant Shirley Henshel to Palmer's store on a fact-finding mission, and her visit paid two dividends. First, she convinced *Look* magazine to do a story on slot car races (July 3, 1962). More importantly, Silverstein used Palmer's event as inspiration for Aurora's own series of sponsored hobby shop races. He hired Palmer as a consultant for $50 a month ("Enough to pay for your hockey tickets," said Silverstein) and began planning what would become the Grand National.

Starting in October 1961, Palmer and four other retailers conducted test competitions. The following month Palmer took several Aurora cars modified by his most successful racers and showed them on the *Today Show*. NBC's John Chancellor maneuvered the cars around the road and model railroad course with only one car-train collision.

Following the success of the trial races, Aurora announced plans for a national racing program. Silverstein declared, "I think we're onto something big." He traveled to Detroit to enlist Ford Motor Corporation as co-sponsor. "This was a hard sell, because not only did I want to use their name—I wanted $100,000 a year from them." He spent the day being passed from one department to another—advertising, marketing, youth division, public relations. "Finally they sat me down and said they have a guy coming in. So he walked in, put his feet on the desk, and said, 'All right, talk for five minutes.'" Silverstein pitched, and the Ford executive smiled. "I love it; it's a go." The guy with his feet on the desk was Lee Iacocca, father of the Ford Mustang and the Ford-Aurora Grand National.

Silverstein instructed Palmer and Schwarzchild to design a program the average shopkeeper could run without undue disruption to store routine. The result was a nine-week series requiring only two hours a week. Palmer designed a standard race course with one long straightaway and a three-curve backstretch. The layout rewarded kids who could soup-up their cars for top-end speed and those who could steer through tight curves. Palmer named it the "Mille Miglia" after the famous Italian "thousand mile" auto race. It fit on a standard display counter and could be stood up behind a door when not in use.

Aware that summer months are traditionally the doldrums for hobby retailers, Aurora scheduled races for June and July. Race packets included a rule book, two trophies, window streamers, pennants, Ford "406" decals—which racers were required to stick on their cars—score sheets, and Model Motoring club cards. Although Aurora later claimed that 5,000 stores took part in the Grand National, Palmer estimated the actual number at 500. Still, the Grand National ended up being the most innovative store promotion of all time.

A trophy from the 1962 Grand National race promotion package sent to participating hobby shops.

Aurora kept the competition keen. And because of their deep-pocketed sponsor, it remained exclusively Ford. The rules stated:

- Only five cars could be used—the Galaxie 500 Sunliner, Galaxie 500 Club Victoria, Country Squire Station Wagon, Ford F-100 pickup, and the Police Car (1548 through 1552). (As it turned out, the Sunliner convertible was the most successful racer, because of its low center of gravity.)
- Race contestants could tune the vibrator motor (a very important consideration).
- Two local celebrity witnesses must certify the official time.
- Forty-eight state winners would be culled from all store winners.
- Eight regional competitions determined the eight finalists who went to New York.

Toots Shors' Restaurant in New York City hosted the preliminary finals on August 20, 1962. Palmer did not want the winner to be decided by some fluke, so he had each contestant race fourteen times over three different courses: a 40-foot drag strip (20 percent of the total point value); a twisting rally course with one full stop (30 percent); and the Mille Miglia course (50 percent).

The leader after one evening of competition was Henry Harnish, the teen who began his career by winning at Palmer's own store. This was a bit of an embarrassment to Palmer, but he declared Harnish had received no special favors. Harnish did not always win his heats, but he finished at or near the top most consistently. He had been practicing two hours a day for a solid month before the championship. "This kid had nerves of steel," explained Palmer. While the pressure got to other racers, Harnish's hands were rock-solid.

The final race was broadcast live from Rockefeller Center on national television during the next morning's Today show. Young Henry dominated, lapping the other three finalists in a 20-lap Mille Miglia race. Ford offered a new 1962 Thunderbird as grand prize—or a rain check for one when Henry turned 21. Henry's father took the T-Bird on the spot (as would all future winners).

The Grand National probably did more to establish slot cars as part of the American consciousness than any other promotion. And the best was yet to come.

Henry Harnish races around the Mille Miglia while a jury of home town notables served as timers.

Chapter Two

THUNDERJETS: The New Generation

This early Thunderjet 500 racing set by Aurora's Netherlands subsidiary came with only one car.

In 1962 slot car mania swept the country. Trade journals reported sales of model railroad items down, while slot car manufacturers couldn't keep pace with demand. "Frankly," said one retailer, "racing cars overpower everything else we sell." More than 20 companies marketed slot car sets in 1962, but most of them sold the larger 1/32 or 1/24 scale units. Aurora did have competition in HO, however: Atlas, Lionel, Marx, and Tyco—all model train manufacturers, to one degree or another, attempting to diversify in the face of stiff slot car competition.

Derek Brand considered Marx Aurora's best challenger. The toy industry's value-pricing leader had developed a small DC motor that worked well and was inexpensive. Still, Marx cars sold for $3.95 at a time when Aurora's sold for $2.49—an obvious burden for the frugal Marx marketeers to bear. Perhaps most important to kids was the simple fact that Aurora cars were faster.

Aurora outsold Marx and all other HO producers combined. Polls revealed that virtually all hobby retailers stocked Aurora slot car products—an astounding fact and strong testimony to Aurora's dominance in the marketplace. Strombecker (maker of 1/32 and 1/24 cars) was a distant second, with Atlas, Scalextric (1/30), and Tyco trailing. Aurora had firmly established itself as the industry leader.

Early Thunderjets: Ford Galaxie convertible (1351 $125), Ford Galaxie hardtop (1352 $125), Ford Falcon hardtop (1354 $90), Thunderbird convertible (1355 $200), Chevy Corvette Stingray (1356 $70), Buick Riviera (1357 $45), Jaguar XKE (1358 $40), and Ford Fairlane hardtop (1353 $110).

The Thunderjet 500

Despite its commanding lead, Aurora understood that slot cars were a rapidly evolving product. Intense competition would ultimately expose the weak link in Aurora's system—the vibrator motor. Even Brand felt his creation was "not a very good motor." In addition to mechanical shortcomings, the AC-powered vibrator played havoc with television reception—not a popular characteristic with parents.

Aurora marketing maven Bill Silverstein and the Hop Up Kits had bought the necessary time for Derek Brand to develop the next-generation power plant for Aurora slot cars. Brand thought he'd found the answer: a new DC motor with two fixed magnets and a conventional armature. He built his prototype at Crafco's workshop in California using magnets he ground into shape by hand, electrical contacts from a washing machine, and a commutator made with a Formica chip pried from his desktop. He installed the prototype in a car and airmailed it to West Hempstead for inspection. One of the R&D team members placed the car on a standard Aurora vibrator layout and instantly burned up the DC motor with alternating current. Aurora R&D staff didn't grasp what had happened—something of an interesting commentary in itself—and simply mailed the dead motor back to Crafco.

Derek Brand saw the burnt armature and immediately knew what had happened. He got the motor working again and planned another showing for Aurora management. On his next New York visit, the subject of the new motor came up as Brand and sales director John Cuomo fished off Long Island. Cuomo mentioned that retailers were still complaining about the vibrator motor, and Brand said he had the solution in his suitcase.

This time Brand was in charge when his prototype was tested, and the results were quite different. Joe Giammarino was pleased. He later declared, "He was quite a guy, that Derek Brand. I liked him a lot. When I first saw him I said, 'You've got to come to work for me.'" Giammarino, the no-nonsense engineer, had found a kindred spirit.

Joe Giammarino contacted Carl Robinette and proclaimed that Derek Brand's talents could be put to better use in New York. Robinette agreed, and Brand moved from Santa Barbara to West Hempstead. (Brand never fully accepted living in New York and refused to purchase a winter overcoat.)

Brand established a Model Motoring lab upstairs at the factory, across the hall from Giammarino's office. There he and ten assistants worked from eight in the morning until seven-thirty at night. They developed new track sections, electrical components, and patterns for car bodies.

Brand and Giammarino immediately began working feverishly to bring the new motor into production. Brand did most of the design, but Giammarino was a man of strong opinions and plenty of manufacturing experience. Production manager Frank Carver tracked down sources for components, going as far as Switzerland to find top-quality gears.

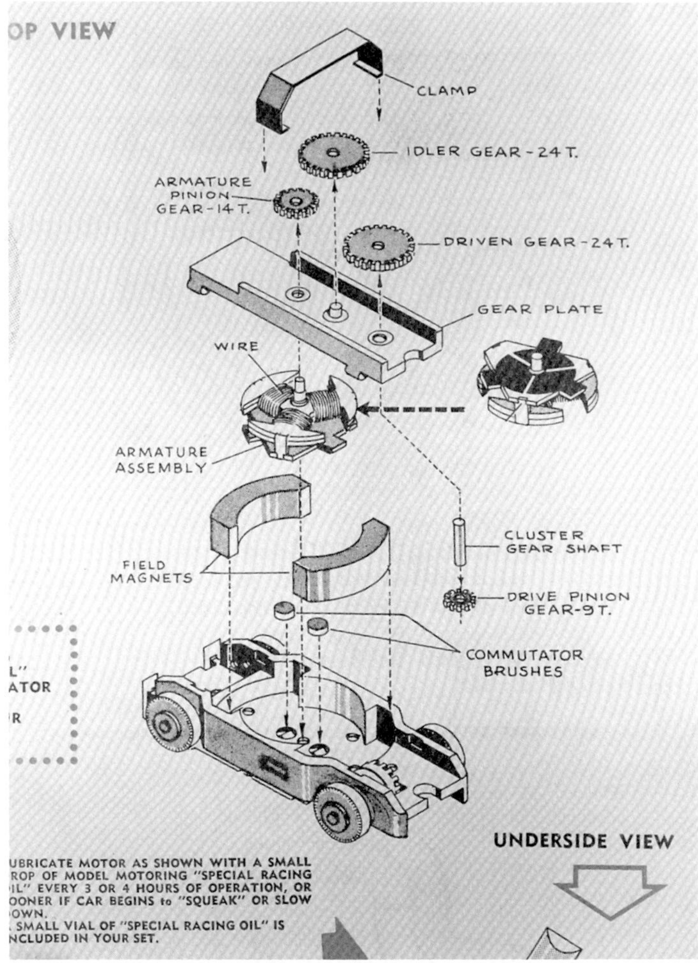

The Thunderjet motor featured a low-profile "pancake" layout and an over-the-top multiple gear linkage to get power to the rear axle.

The new motor design was innovative and worthy of a patent. At first Aurora's attorney was skeptical, but he succeeded in obtaining a patent for the new engine. The names of Brand and Giammarino were assigned to patent number 3,243,917.

The result was best summarized by Aurora advertising: "A new miracle motor... it will outperform every other slot-car motor on the market, by any standard you can dream up." In a stroke of brand-concepting brilliance, Silverstein named it the "Thunderjet 500." The hype continued: "Laboratory tests prove a Model Motoring car with a T-jet 500 under the hood will exceed the speed of sound in scale miles per hour." Who could resist such a claim?

No one, as it turned out. Aurora unveiled the Thunderjet 500 motor at the 1963 HIAA convention and it was the hit of the show—except with Aurora's competitors. The T-jet was twice as fast as the vibrator, nearly three times as fast as Marx, more than twice as fast as Tyco, and about 25 percent faster than Aurora's nearest competitor, Eldon. (Faller of Germany quickly copied the T-jet, and in Brand's opinion, "did a fine job." Aurora agreed not to sue Faller as long as they kept their product out of the United States market.) Jose Rodriguez, Jr., reviewing the Thunderjet 500 for *Car Model* magazine (July 1963) declared it the best motor he'd ever seen. Derek Brand had once again delivered a knockout punch for Aurora.

Innovation in Design

The most obvious innovation was the Thunderjet 500's design. A conventional motor employs a rotating armature and magnets encased in a metal can. Competitors mounted their motors horizontally—on the motor's side—so that the motor drive shaft extending outward would drive the rear-axle gear, propelling the car forward.

The Thunderjet took that concept and turned it on its end—literally. The T-jet motor sat upright in the chassis. Its drive shaft extended from the top of the motor, giving it a flattened look Brand dubbed the "pancake." This lowered the car's center of gravity and added an even greater performance advantage.

The T-jet's drive train was also a complete departure from standard slot car design. While a typical can motor transferred power with a simple two-gear arrangement, the T-jet required a five-gear linkage to deliver power from the drive shaft, across the top of the motor, and down to the rear axle. It sounds complicated, but it was actually quite simple and extremely effective.

There were many more-subtle innovations within the Thunderjet, but the most obvious was its oversized armature. Since it was clear slot cars would not play a part in HO railroading, Brand was free to increase motor size. The chassis was widened and lengthened. Cars were now closer to 1/80 than 1/87 in scale, but everyone agreed it was a positive change: the cars were easier to assemble and better for hobbyist tinkering.

Aurora also enlarged the steering wheel controller to make it easier to handle. Designers added two new features: a direction-reverse switch and a "brake" that cut track power. Racers like Henry Harnish discovered that the brake was better for slowing at curves than turning down power. Kids who raced Aurora cars and used Aurora controllers had an obvious advantage over their competitors, and Aurora advertising of the day drove that point home, time and time again. You either raced Aurora, or you came in second.

End of the Vibrator Road

The debut of Thunderjets meant death for vibrators. Old stock remained in stores for a while, and some hobbyists still enjoyed tinkering with them. However, after production of a million and a half copies, vibrator mechanisms were soon history. And because vibrator car bodies were too small for the larger T-jet chassis, all but four were discontinued. The survivors through modification: Hot Rods (1553 and 1554) and the Mack Dump and Stake Truck (1582 and 1583). Aurora also converted the International Semi (1580) into a tow truck (1364).

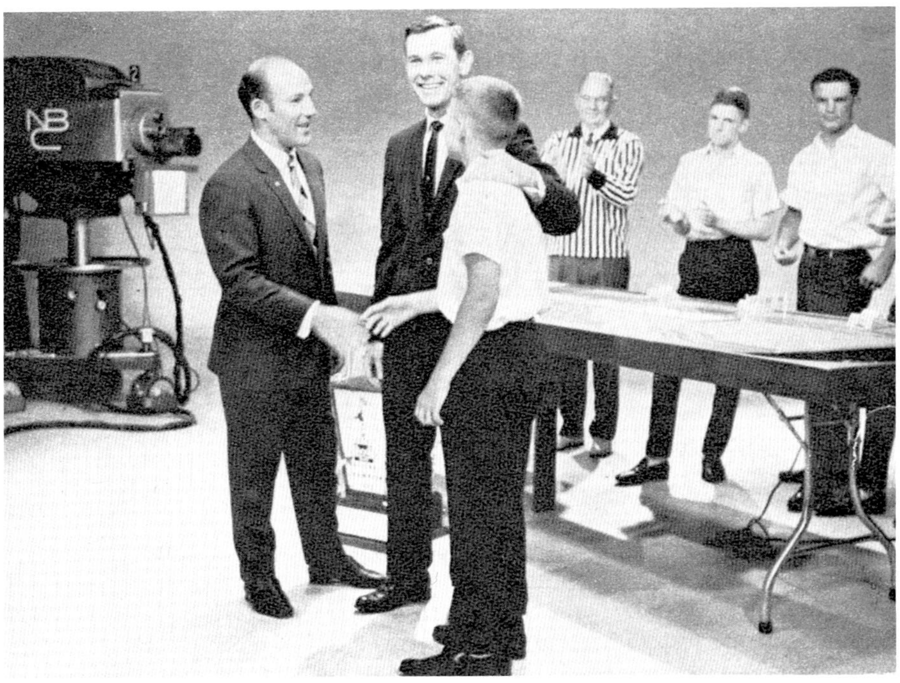

Sterling Moss (left) congratulates 1963 Grand National champ Ronnie Colerick as the Tonight Show's Johnny Carson jokes with the audience. *Rod & Custom Models.*

The price of the new cars continued to creep up. Back in 1961 a vibrator car sold for $1.98 and a truck for $2.49. The Thunderjet equivalents were $2.98 and $3.49. However, thereafter Aurora managed to hold the line on prices pretty well for the rest of the 1960s. Slot cars weren't cheap, but a typical boy could afford to accumulate quite a collection over a couple of years. Aurora wanted its customers to come back for more of its products; thus it continued to add to its growing lineup of new Thunderjet models. The temptation to buy the latest T-jet in the hobby shop display case was usually irresistible.

It seems amazing in today's market-research-dominated world of manufacture, but in the early 1960s, selecting new cars for Model Motoring hinged almost completely on what the men in the plant liked and thought would sell. At weekly sandwich and coke lunch meetings Brand, other staffers, and managers sat around and traded ideas. At one point both Giammarino and Shikes were driving Buick Rivieras—so naturally that became an Aurora slot car.

The R&D team began the production process by gathering photographs supplied by auto manufacturers (especially Ford) and pictures from car magazines. Draftsmen then produced engineering drawings from which Brand carved his body prototypes. He shaped his patterns in sugar pine three times the size of the actual HO body. It took only a week to complete a body prototype.

Aurora relied on outside toolmakers to produce their slot car body molds. More often than not, finished patterns were sent to Ace Tool & Die in Newark, New Jersey, where Aurora's model kit steel production molds also were cut. Ace would use a pantograph machine to reduce the scale of the pattern down to HO size as the mold was cut. When complete, the tools were delivered to West Hempstead and production commenced.

Meanwhile, Derek Brand was only one man, and Aurora needed more automotive variety than he alone could design. To enhance development, Aurora occasionally turned to HMS, the Willow Grove, Pennsylvania, company that designed Aurora model kits, including the now-classic monster figure kits. HMS technicians carved patterns in acetate, a medium that is easier to use than wood but less stable. Interestingly, HMS generally carved its patterns in exact HO scale, a practice that limited detail.

HMS patterns went to Ferriot Brothers in Toledo, Ohio, for tool production. Ferriot manufactured Aurora figure kit tooling, as well as molds for Marx playset figures. Unlike the cut-steel molds produced by Ace, Ferriot made tooling by using the lost-wax method to directly cast the patterns into beryllium copper molds. The result: a quicker and less expensive production tool. Aurora did not mess around, and bringing a new car body into production took only about three months.

Production, of course, was concentrated at West Hempstead. At first Aurora's standard molding machines did all the work, producing bodies from four-cavity molds. However, after a few years Giammarino switched to smaller German-made Arburg machines. The Arburgs molded only one body at a time, but they were fully automated; one worker could tend several machines, and, in Joe Giammarino's words, they "went like jackrabbits."

The Magic of Aurora Marketing

To promote the new Thunderjets Aurora went to the world of real racing and found a celebrity spokesman—world class grand prix driver Sterling Moss. Bill Silverstein traveled to England to recruit Moss and was exceedingly pleased with the outcome. "He was terrific," explained Silverstein. The personable, charming Moss added both a touch of European class and authentic sporting feel to slot racing, which, declared Moss in Aurora ads, "is incredible, quite like actual racing." Moss had one other important qualification in Silverstein's eyes: after a wreck in 1962, Moss had retired from racing. Aurora's high-profile public representative would not be dying in an accident. The action photo of Sterling Moss that went on the new Thunderjet catalog quickly became an indelible symbol of Model Motoring in the minds of America's boys.

Moss's first important assignment was serving as Chief Steward of the Second Ford-Aurora Grand National Model Motoring Championship in 1963. Ford dealers across the country joined in the promotion because they thought the miniature electric cars generated public interest in Ford's full-size cars. And hobby shops loved it because people saw free advertising for their shops at their local Ford dealerships.

Aurora retained the same basic format for the Second Grand National, but some changes enhanced the competition: Aurora added two more trophies to the dealer race package and included a cardboard "Used Car Lot" display. The idea was for dealers to take old cars as partial payment for new ones, then resell the old cars to enthusiasts. Entrants received a "427" decal to place on their cars. Any of Aurora's Ford cars could be raced, except for the Hot Rods (1553, 1554) with their wide "racing slick" rear tires. The final change: the eight national finalists were selected from time trials, eliminating regional competitions and the need for contestant travel.

The Grand National championship was staged in the Mercury Ballroom of the New York Hilton, with more than 200 spectators watching the action on the three drag, rally, and Mille Miglia tracks. Comfortable in his new role, Sterling Moss mingled with the crowd. *Car Model* magazine's L. T. Shaw (November 1963) found him "a warm, friendly man, intensely interested in all aspects of the contest and extremely easy to talk to." Shaw also noted the crowd's enthusiasm: "I overheard one boy's mother explain the differences between vibrator motors and the new Thunderjet 500 to a curious bystander as calmly (and correctly) as if she were discussing a cake recipe."

The four best drivers appeared for the final race on the August 20 *Tonight Show.* The slowest qualifier was twelve-year-old Ronnie Colerick of Rapid City, South Dakota, who was assigned lane one after the other drivers had picked their lanes. The race started with wild spinouts by all four drivers, but Colerick settled down and pulled away from the other boys. The race became a runaway when the others were pressed into mistakes while trying to catch up.

Indianapolis racers in regular (1359 $80) as well as silver and gold chrome (1360 $40). Also, Grand Prix racer (1361 $35), along with Mack Dump (1362 $75), Mack Stake (1363 $70), and International Wrecker (1364). The red/black Wrecker ($60) is fairly common, the white/yellow/red version ($300) is rare, while the very scarce red/white ($400) early issue still has the horn on the roof held over in the transition from the Vibrator International Truck Tractor.

Colerick explained that he was less affected by the pressure of the televised race because he was too young to appreciate what was at stake. His dad owned a hobby shop, and Ronnie had spent up to five hours a day honing his driving skills. When host Johnny Carson presented Colerick with his trophy and 1963 Ford Thunderbird, Ronnie exclaimed "Neat, man! I'll let my dad drive it sometimes." Carson quipped, "You mean he wins a Thunderbird for that?!" Carson's flippant dismissal of slot car racing elicited the anger of *Car Model*'s Shaw, who thought all the TV hoopla detracted from the seriousness of the competition. (Bill Silverstein's greatest regret was that ABC's *Wide World of Sports* refused to carry the Grand National, saying it wasn't a real sport.)

The Need for Standards

Slot car racing's popularity was growing beyond the basic home road racing set. Aurora's Grand National was nationally known, and competitions sponsored by other manufacturers, clubs, and model car magazines vied for attention. While the vast majority of racing sets were sold for home use by kids, a growing number of hobbyists were transforming slot racing into a sport. Aurora president Abe Shikes saw this as another potential market. Consultants Rich Palmer and Dick Schwarzchild approached Shikes with the idea of founding a national slot racing association.

Abe Shikes supported the concept. The result: the Miniature International Racing Association (MINRA). Shikes put up $20,000 to launch the organization, but Aurora's connection was kept secret and Shikes left operations to his consultants. Initially, MINRA's official headquarters was in Englewood, New Jersey, but after a few months it was moved to an office at the back of Palmer's store. Homer Leovas, a well-known Sports Car Club of America driver and officer, was named executive director.

Like any sanctioning association, MINRA's mission was to establish order and uniformity to the infant sport of slot car racing. Before MINRA, each manufacturer and racing organization set its own standards and made

Hot Rod roadster (1365 $75) and coupe (1366 $300) on the track. On the right: Maserati (1367 $40), with and without stripe, and Ferrari GTO (1368 $45). On the left: classic Lincoln Continental (1369 $60) and AC Cobra (1370 $80) with pre-production test shot of the body in translucent plastic.

its own rules. The result was chaos. For the sport to grow, it needed a national organization, and Aurora hoped MINRA would be that organization.

Homer Leovas models a MINRA T-shirt.

At the 1963 HIAA national convention Leovas spoke about MINRA, and Aurora's John Cuomo, chairman of the HIAA slot car committee, urged hobby shops to set up race centers along MINRA guidelines. Leovas said MINRA would produce a rule book setting standards for layouts, race management, and car classifications. It would also begin publishing *In the Groove*, a newsletter for the slot car community. MINRA would supply mail-order trophies and other items necessary for a top-quality race. MINRA members would receive *In the Groove*, a membership card, and a club pin. It was a well-formed concept that deserved support.

In the Groove's first issue appeared in February 1963. Considering its hidden benefactor, the newspaper was remarkably evenhanded in its treatment of manufacturers other than Aurora. MINRA sponsored its first national championship contest—a drag race—at Schwarzchild's Kingston, Pennsylvania, shop. Unlike Aurora's Grand National, there was a twist: competitors mailed their cars to Schwarzchild's shop, where they were raced by MINRA's team of experienced slot racers. The fastest car was Gene Wagner's HO Thunderjet-powered Corvette, which covered the scale half-mile in just 2.451 seconds—820 scale miles per hour. Aurora was so pleased it reported the accomplishment in its 1964 catalog.

Beat the Champ

The ill-fated Beat the Champ competition had all the makings of a surefire promotional winner.

In 1964 Bill Silverstein decided to revamp the Third Annual Ford-Aurora Grand National because many hobby dealers were losing their enthusiasm for in-store racing. Silverstein streamlined the contest to reduce the hassles of managing the races. His clever idea was Beat the Champ, a simple two-week long contest in which seven regional winners would be determined by time trials alone.

The official Grand National track was an 18 by 66 inch oval that duplicated Ford's Dearborn test track, with its long straightaways that twisted in shallow turns. Silverstein selected Aurora's models of the new Ford Mustang hardtop and convertible as the official competition cars—meaning hobby shop dealers could expect sales to race participants. To emphasize driving skill and minimize hop-up cleverness, contestants were required to use stock cars that could be could be tuned but not modified. Those who reached the finals would receive Aurora Mustangs upon arrival in New York, giving them just 24 hours to adjust the cars to their liking.

The other key ingredient in the program required having a champion race car driver establish a thirty-lap time trial standard for contestants to beat on their local hobby shop track. Those who did would receive gold-plated Ford Mustang pins. Silverstein made a fateful decision to pass over Stirling Moss and select an active racing star as official "Champ." His choice was NASCAR all-time money winner Glenn "Fireball" Roberts.

Kids who could beat Fireball Roberts' time would have earned a gold-plated stopwatch/ Mustang pin.

Roberts flew to Dearborn and kicked off Beat the Champ at a reception for Ford executives and hobby industry representatives. Following the gathering, he flew to Charlotte, North Carolina, for the annual 600-mile NASCAR event. Seven minutes into the race, a car spun out ahead of Roberts. His car sideswiped another, veered into the infield, flipped, and burst into flames. A fellow driver pulled Roberts from the wreckage, but Aurora's contest spokesman was burned over 70 percent of his body because he had refused to wear a fireproof suit. He died five weeks later.

The accident devastated Aurora's contest and advertising program. Immediately upon hearing of the accident, Aurora canceled Beat the Champ and terminated all publicity featuring Roberts' name. Silverstein had been right the first time when he signed Moss: retired legends don't die on race tracks in the middle of promotions.

Because of Roberts' untimely demise, Grand National time trials weren't held until early fall—and in a greatly revised format. On October 6 the fastest drivers from each state went to their local dealers for the final trial. At 4:30 Eastern Time the command "Go!" was issued via telephone from Aurora headquarters, and all forty-eight races started simultaneously. Each store had three independent timers to verify results, and Aurora required winning cars be impounded to make sure (in Palmer's words) "nobody had been Mickey Mousing around with the car."

Steve Allen (center, rear) and Stirling Moss keep a watchful eye over Grand National finalists during an *I've Got a Secret* Aurora racing interlude. Tom Kilduff (no. 1) took top honors and a new Mustang.

On Saturday, November 13, the seven regional finalists assembled with their parents at the New York Hilton. Silverstein handed out their official race shirts and went over the competition rules; then they all sat down together for dinner. Sunday was devoted to a series of races over four different tracks that narrowed the field down to the final four. After Sunday's races, preliminaries leader Tom Kilduff of Kingston, Pennsylvania, went back to his hotel room and practiced some more on the track he brought with him to the competition.

Monday the finalists had breakfast together, then went off to CBS studios to tape Steve Allen's *I've Got a Secret* CBS game show. The boys' secret: "One of us is going to win $5,000 tonight." Once the quiz was finished, the contestants moved to the stage where Derek Brand and his crew had set up the race course. Stirling Moss officiated. As points leader, Kilduff got to pick his lane first, and he chose the outside lane. From there he proceeded to win the final race, a new Ford Mustang, and a $2,000 college scholarship.

Super Model Motoring: The 1/48 Scale Wrong Turn

HMS's original pattern of the '31 Ford Pickup (1751) came with a roll bar, not the roof included with the sales version.

Craftsmen at HMS gave the '49 Mercury drag strip embellishments designed to set kids' imaginations in motion.

Just a week after the Grand National finals, the National Custom Car Show opened in New York City. As was typical for the time, model and slot car manufacturers had booths alongside real-life cars. Aurora had big news for the automotive world: the debut of Super Model Motoring, slot cars in 1/48 scale. "Not too big ... not too small, but sized right in between."

In basic terms, Super Model Motoring attempted to find an unoccupied niche between small HO cars and large 1/32 and 1/24 systems. Joe Giammarino even hoped Lionel railroaders would support the size-compatible line. Although Super Model Motoring cars had a new, larger chassis, their motor was the same T-jet found in Aurora HO cars. Body styles designed by HMS were all in the hot rod vein: a '31 Model A pickup, '32 Ford Sedan, '36 Ford convertible, and '57 Chevy hardtop (1751 through 1754). Aurora launched Super Model Motoring with two sets, one at $24.95 and the other at $29.95, complete with an overpass to construct an over-under figure eight. There were no other accessories. Given the limited variety, Aurora's entry into O gauge racing looked timid.

The hobby industry didn't know what to make of the 1/48 cars. Jose Rodriguez, Jr., of *Car Model* liked the line, but asked the essential question, "Do we need another scale?" Others criticized the cars' lack of detail and accurate proportioning. The T-jet motor generated plenty of power, but the fundamental issue remained: Who wanted them?

Super Model Motoring, in all its ill-fated glory, clockwise from top: 1931 Ford pickup (1751 $60), 1957 Thunderbird (1756 $80), 1932 Deuce Rod (1758 $65), 1949 Mercury coupe (1755 $60), 1932 Ford chopped sedan (1752 $60), 1936 Ford convertible (1753 $60), 1927 Ford T (1757 $60), 1957 Chevy (1754 $120).

During 1964 Aurora added four more "rods" to the line: a 1947 Mercury, 1957 Thunderbird, 1932 Ford Deuce, and 1927 Model T rod (1755 through 1758). However, it did not help. Sales were terrible, and Aurora decided to let the line die quietly. "We couldn't give them away," observed Brand, who thought hot rods had limited appeal. Proving you do only live twice, Aurora disposed of its surplus inventory of 1/48 chassis by selling them to the A. C. Gilbert Company, which used them in a James Bond spy slot car set.

If Only, If Only ...

The sudden death of Super Model Motoring had a lasting impact, little noticed at the time. The line's untimely demise kept Aurora from issuing a handful of cars that would have become certain collectors' classics today: the Monstermobiles.

The line that never launched: Monstermobiles, slot cars based on Aurora's hybrid hot rod and monster plastic figure kits like Frankenstein's Flivver, Dracula's Dragster, and King Kong's Thronester (Shown here and on following page).

1964 was the year of monster mania in America. *The Addams Family* and *The Munsters* cavorted across the nation's television screens, and Aurora sold Universal Movie Monster figure kits like crazy. Aurora R&D team members designed patterns for at least three cars driven by popular monsters: Frankenstein, Dracula, and King Kong. The cars were miniature versions of popular Aurora model kits depicting monsters driving hot rods. Aurora even issued a press release announcing the cars, but never produced them. Today, photographs are all that remain of what might have been some of the most collectible slot cars ever manufactured.

Grand National Competition Pac. Three regular-issue Mustangs: convertible (1371 $110), standard coupe (1372 $100), and 2+2 fastback (1373 $300); plus two candy-colored fastback shells (1501 $400).

Leadership

Despite the 1/48 setback, HO slot car popularity surged. By 1965 HO Model Motoring was a staple in the toy and hobby industry. Indeed, the enormous popularity of slot cars had made Aurora Plastics Corporation the largest hobby company in the world—an incredible achievement in such a short period of time. The Thunderjet motor was powerful enough to keep slot enthusiasts happy and reliable enough to be a hit in the mass market. Marx and Lionel dropped out, leaving just Tyco and Atlas to compete for leftovers.

Candy Colors, in early painted and later plated versions. From left: Jaguar XKE (1392 $60, $45), Ford GT (1395 $60, $45), Corvette Stingray (1391 $75, $50), Grand Prix racer (1393 $60, $45), Ferrari 250 GTO (1394 $60, $45), and Cobra GT (1396 $60, $45).

Mid-1960s Thunderjet set boxes featured the Ford Mustang, then America's best-selling vehicle.

1965 wasn't a major year for innovation at Aurora. The only novel introduction was cosmetic—painting six models in brilliant "Candy Colors" (1391 through 1396). Later, Aurora would plate these same cars in candy-colored chrome. Aurora also produced some new track products, but these too were largely cosmetic.

The most spectacular new item—"Cobra Climb" Spiral Roadway Support (1594), a base and pedestal with arms that tilted curved track sections up, into a 360-degree spiral, then down.

Five other track accessories also appeared, the most interesting to serious racers being the Corner Crossover (1513). Racers had asked for this segment, because it sent cars into opposite lanes on a curve, following the path that centrifugal force would compel real cars to follow on a race course.

After the tragedy of Fireball Roberts, the 1965 Ford-Aurora Grand National returned to the weekly in-store race format. This time America's best known road course driver Dan Gurney served as celebrity race marshal. To encourage hobby shop owners to participate, Aurora handed out merchandise prizes to stores that promoted the contest well, even if their store did not produce a winning racer. Entrants had to purchase candy plated red, blue, or green Mustang 2+2 (1373) cars to run in the contest. Local competitions took place in June and regional run-offs brought eight finalists to Aurora's massive new Raceway Center in West Hempstead on December 9. There were five preliminary race courses, and for the first time, they included competition for the increasingly popular 1/32 and 1/25 cars. This was Aurora's contest, however, and the HO races carried the most importance.

The next day, after completion of the opening rounds, Aurora management and the top four contestants drove to Philadelphia. The final race was held on *The Mike Douglas Show.* John Seeley of Rapid City duplicated the feat of his neighbor (and 1963 winner) Ronnie Colerick by driving a Mustang 2+2 to victory. Rich Palmer observed that Rapid City's two wins showed what could happen when slot racing caught on in a community (although South Dakota's long winters may have had something to do with it, too!). World land speed record-holder Craig Breedlove presented Seeley with a trophy and keys to a real Mustang 2+2.

The Mike Douglas Show hosted the 1965 Grand National finals. Terry-Thomas, Ethel Merman, and Dan Dailey watched from the set. Aurora's Rich Palmer (left) and Dick Schwarzchild served as race officials.

Chapter Three
SCALE: Battle for Supremacy

The slot car boom of the early 1960s is defined in two letters: HO. This one scale dominated sales and outsold larger-scale cars by a huge margin. However, HO sets were primarily the domain of the mass-market starter sets generally sold to and for children.

As the decade progressed, older teen and adult interest in slot cars took a different turn as they found big slot car racing to be a more challenging hobby. The larger scale cars more easily lent themselves to custom modifications designed to enhance race performance. Manufacturers of larger-scale cars and after-market speed equipment accessories began to offer products with appeal to hard-core, mature hobbyists. 1/32 and 1/24 scale cars zoomed into popularity in the mid-1960s, leading to a secondary slot explosion—a boom that remained largely separate from the HO car universe.

Craft, Model and Hobby Industry filled its pages with articles telling hobby retailers how to cash in on the raceway bonanza. An early lesson learned was that noisy raceways didn't mix with retail hobby shop environments. Dealers, however, could recoup the overhead of a separate facility by renting track time at 50 cents a half-hour and cars for 25 cents. Raceways invariably included a kit and parts counter where racers could buy cars and supplies. Coke and candy machines added to the potential for profits.

There were two kinds of raceways: bare-bones, concrete-floored facilities for serious racers and plush, carpeted "family entertainment centers" for the broader casual market. However, dealers who hoped to lure girl customers into their centers soon discovered business was almost all male, with the 15-year-old boy dominating the demographic profile.

Aurora's Dick Schwarzchild and Bill Silverstein with racing legend Carroll Shelby (right) at Aurora's raceway.

The American Classic set was designed for fun racing at home, not hobby racing at a commercial slot car center.

Rise of the Raceway

Since larger slot layouts didn't fit into most homes, commercial raceways were the favored answer. Like so many trends, slot car parlors showed up first in California—the earliest opening in 1961 in Los Angeles. Two years later, there were 30 raceways, nearly all in the Los Angeles area. And by 1964, the boom had jumped the Rocky Mountains into metropolitan centers of the Midwest and East.

The heady, early days of slot raceways did produce some notes of caution from veteran hobby industry observers. *Craft, Model and Hobby* reminded readers of the trampoline center craze a few years earlier, warning that slot car parlors might be another "bubble." A Californian writing to *Model Car & Track* in the November 1964 issue noted, "Out here there are too many tracks—on nearly as many street corners as filling stations. Some will live and some won't." However, others contended that outside big cities, America was largely unaware of slot car racing and predicted raceway growth was only just beginning.

Aurora management felt that their leadership role in slot cars demanded they too get into the raceway business—and do it in a very big way. Aurora purchased an old Vic Tanny gym down the block from the West Hempstead factory. Dick Schwarzchild, who had been brought in-house as Bill Silverstein's sales and promotion assistant, was given the task of setting up the new raceway.

However, Schwarzchild was skeptical of the long-term success of slot raceways. He observed that average drivers spent too much time retrieving crashed cars from the floor and returning them to the track—a bad omen.

Silverstein made sure the raceway's July 22, 1965, grand opening was a national event. He assembled 40 reporters at the Manhattan Biltmore and put them on a chartered coach to West Hempstead—along with a caterer, plenty of food, and a few Broadway chorus girls. Five of the East Coast's top slot racers were on hand to demonstrate their skills. Aurora declared the Raceway Center their new proving grounds—their way of keeping a finger on the pulse of the hobby.

The reluctant Schwarzchild had done a terrific job. Nine large tracks—seven for large-scale cars, two for HO, each with color-coded lanes—filled the 16,000-square-foot center. Modern swivel chairs enhanced racers' comfort. Walls featured large photos of race cars in action. The hobby shop carried the latest cars and equipment by all major manufacturers, not just Aurora. How could it not thrive?

The Mustang 350GT (3253 $60) and Pontiac GTO (3252 $60) epitomized America's love for sporty cars in the 1960s. They were the most common cars in Aurora's A-Jet homes race sets.

The Move into Large Scale

Joe Giammarino recalled that Aurora felt obliged to get involved in the booming big-car market rather than forfeiting it to the competition. "Where we could make a buck, we'd make it," he recalled. Derek Brand added, "Revell had a 1/32 system, and we looked at it enviously and said, 'If they can do it, we can do it.'"

Bill Silverstein shared Schwarzchild's reservations about large slot cars. He felt that going into large cars diluted Aurora's commitment to HO. Indeed, it went against Model Motoring's slogans, "Twice the race in half the space" and "More zoom in less room." Aurora

Aurora and K&B 1/32 cars. Back row from the left: Mustang (3253 $60), Comet (3258 $75), Pontiac (3252 $60), Corvair (3254 $75), and Barracuda (3255 $75). Front row from the left: Chaparral (3256 $75), Lola (3259 $80), Ford GT (3251 $75), and Cobra (3257 $75).

nonetheless gave its new 1/32 cars top billing at the 1965 HIAA convention.

Called Aurora Americans A-Jets, the cars were marketed like their HO counterparts—as ready-to-run cars in packaged sets for the home, not specialty cars for the slot enthusiast. Dan Gurney signed on as A-Jets spokesman. Aurora initially offered ten sports and Grand Prix body styles, all featuring large American flag stickers on their doors. The two basic sets sold for $39.95 and $49.95—quite an investment for a Christmas toy.

Interestingly, A-Jets' running gear was partly derivative, partly original. In a nod to compatibility, Aurora mounted the braided-metal pickups on either side of the guide blade, like all other 1/32 cars. It meant that A-Jets would run on anyone's track.

Originality, however, was not lacking. Aurora's aluminum chassis was a West Hempstead creation, just as the innovative Challenger sidewinder motor (3250) was. The new motor was pure Derek Brand. He took a T-jet motor, turned it on its side, and enlarged the components, but its three-pole armature and distinctively shaped magnets revealed its T-jet heritage. The Challenger was packaged in a unique snap-together metal and plastic casing that made it easy to access and work on. Aurora built the new motor in West Hempstead.

The Challenger was different from the in-line can motors installed in about 80% of competitive cars. Rather than having the drive shaft come out the rear of the motor and link to the rear axle gear, the Challenger was mounted sideways right above the rear axle, with the drive shaft linking the rear axle from the side. This sidewinder arrangement placed the weight of the motor directly over the rear wheels for better traction. In fact, the Challenger came with a threaded axle built in.

Despite its many fine attributes, the Challenger simply could not match the power of other motors. Brand realized from the beginning that the Challenger's power was "just ordinary," so in response to demand for more speed Aurora brought out an improved version—the Super Challenger (1504)—early in 1966. Aurora rewound the Challenger's armatures to transform the 12-volt original into a hot 6-volt power plant that was more competitive with other stock motors on the market.

The K&B Connection

In reality, the A-Jets weren't Aurora's first foray into large-scale slot cars. Since 1963 Aurora's California subsidiary K&B had marketed 1/25 and 1/24 accessories manufactured by a variety of suppliers but sold under the "Model Rama" trademark. The blister packed parts included axles, wheels, chassis, pick-ups, lubricants, and clear vacuum formed bodies. Later K&B added racing tires and controllers to its selection.

Since K&B served the serious hobbyist market, it was compelled to enter the burgeoning "hot motor" field. K&B's first motor, the Bobcat (1501), debuted early in 1965. A large 36D-size can motor, it was manufactured by can-motor giant Mabuchi of Japan. K&B simply jumped on a well-established bandwagon with the Bobcat since

Four versions of the Lola T-70. The Aurora 1/32 scale model kit and A-Jet (3259 $80) on the left used the same body shell as the K&B kit (1833 $200). K&B also released the T-70 in 1/24 scale as a kit (1805 $160) and as the body-only shown here (1805-1 $50).

most American competitors already sold Mabuchi-built motors.

Mabuchi is one of the great success stories of the hobby industry. Founded after World War II by the Mabuchi brothers, Kenichi and Takaichi, Mabuchi was "discovered" by the Polk brothers in the 1950s building motors in a Tokyo shop with a staff of five women. With U.S. distribution handled by the Polks, Mabuchi achieved tremendous success at a time when Americans had negative images of Japanese-made products. By 1965, Mabuchi had four Tokyo plants employing 1500 workers who built 250,000 motors daily. Mabuchi motors powered America's big scale slot car hobby.

K&B president John Brodbeck had known Ken Mabuchi since the mid-1950s. Once when Brodbeck visited Japan to check on the export of K&B gasoline-fueled model airplane motors, he visited Mabuchi and was pleasantly surprised to find that his host was a model airplane buff with a closet full of K&B engines for his personal use. Despite his early relationship with Mabuchi, Brodbeck was not one of the first American hobby manufacturers to sell Mabuchi motors.

Dan Gurney carried the emblem of K&B Aurora into battle at Riverside, California, on his McLaren Mark 2.

In 1965 when K&B first began selling kit slot cars, they did not mount Bobcat motors; instead they used the Aurora-made Challenger motor. K&B's cars also came with the same body shells used by Aurora in the A-jets, but unlike the ready-to-run Aurora cars, K&B's came in kits to be assembled. They were aimed at the slot hobbyist who enjoyed working with his cars and wanted to interchange and modify parts. Because K&B sold the cars as kits, they avoided the labor costs of factory assembly and were marketed at $6.

Aurora's mass-market orientation limited their large-scale releases to intermediate-sized 1/32 cars. This left K&B free to issue cars in larger scales—a natural step, since K&B already marketed 1/24 and 1/25 scale components. In fact, its first 1/25 scale car, the Dragmaster (308), was little more than a metal chassis with a driver's head stuck on top.

K&B's first real 1/25 scale car kits, the Ford GT and Cobra GT (1800 and 1801), were well-received by slot enthusiasts. Their best feature was molded-in clear windows. Other manufacturers' kits required gluing, usually producing ugly smears. K&B retained Ted Neward's contract molding shop in nearby Pomona to design and manufacture integrated clear parts. Neward's process was ingenious: clear windows were first molded separately,

K&B 1/25 and 1/24 kit cars. Back row from the left: Ferrari 250 GTO (1803 $140), Porsche 906 (1802 $130), Cobra (1801 $165), and Ford GT (1800 $160). Front row from the left: Chaparral (1804 $160), Lola (1805 $160), and Ferrari 330 P2 (1806 $250).

then placed into cavities in the body molds before plastic injection. When the cavities filled with molten plastic, heat fused the clear windows to the opaque bodies. Brodbeck rated success in this tricky process one of K&B's greatest accomplishments.

K&B cars ran on an adjustable aluminum chassis, complete with a spring-loaded pick-up arm and realistic, plastic-spoked "aluminum" wheel inserts. The motor was the Challenger sidewinder. Model Car Science (March 1965) declared K&B's product line "different from run-of-the-mill kits."

The major drawback—1/25 scale. Almost every other company had standardized at 1/24, but K&B had inherited 1/25 from parent Aurora, which used that size for its automotive model kits. In fact, the K&B Ford GT used elements from Aurora's model kit. K&B ultimately fell into line, releasing future cars in 1/24.

K&B issued its first pair of 1/24 cars during the summer of 1965, and praise from slot hobbyists was immediate. The Porsche 906/916 and Ferrari 250 GTO (1802,1803) were noted for detailed, lightweight plastic bodies. The Porsche 906 caught some car buffs by surprise. Familiar with the 904, many didn't know Porsche had revamped the car. K&B's design secret was the direct help it had received from Porsche.

The new kits incorporated K&B's latest innovation: the patented Posi-Lok wheel attachment system. Most wheels slipped onto coarsely threaded axles and locked into place with nuts. This usually meant wheels were off-center, sometimes working loose during races. Posi-Lok was simple: wheels stayed in place with a collet—a tapered sleeve you could position anywhere on a smooth axle. Turn a nut, lock the collet, true the wheel position, and your car's tires were locked. For serious racers, this new feature provided a competitive advantage on the racetrack.

Next in the summer of 1965 K&B moved from kit cars into ready-to-race 1/24 scale cars aimed at serious hobbyists who wanted a hot car right out of the box. The new products had Posi-Lok wheels and were powered by various K&B Mabuchi motors. Taking another lesson from the A-Jets, K&B went against convention and mounted its motors sidewinder-style. Because of K&B's slow release schedule, most cars had the prevailing Mabuchi or Aurora motor of the day.

The first in the series, the Ford Lotus 30 Charger (1850), came with the new 9-volt Royal Bobcat (1500). The Cooper F-1 (1851) of early 1966 was powered by a K&B Wildcat (1505). The Cooper was a narrow-bodied, open-wheel Formula I racer, so it took a smaller 16D-size motor mounted in-line. *Model Car Science* tested the 9-volt Wildcat against the Aurora-built 6-volt Super Challenger in May 1966 and found the Challenger had better top-end speed on a long track, while the Wildcat performed better on a short, tight track. In a bow to advanced racers' concerns, K&B converted to vacuum-formed bodies. The reason: cars with injection-molded bodies looked better, but their heavier weight made them too slow for serious racing.

By 1966 slot car sales had increased so much that K&B expanded to two assembly lines running 16 hours a day. Ten thousand cars rolled off these lines daily.

K&B's first two 1/24 cars, the Ferrari 250 GTO (1803 $140) and Porsche 906/916 (1802 $130). Jack Leynnwood, artist for Aurora and Revell plastic model kits, did the fabulous box art.

New York Senator Robert Kennedy examines the Vac-U-Tron device installed in the car of Aurora president Abe Shikes.

At the time K&B had another product with even greater sales potential: an exhaust emissions control device for real cars. Fred Dunn, a K&B engineer, came up with the idea of recycling exhaust back through a car's engine before sending it out the tail pipe. Dunn expected it to boost mileage, but it turned out to be more effective as a pollution control device. Aurora called it Vac-U-Tron and installed it on UPS trucks and California highway patrol cars to demonstrate its effectiveness. Abe Shikes even got his New York congressman to read a letter into the *Congressional Record* praising Aurora's civic mindedness. However, neither the federal or state governments were yet ready to pass laws restricting auto emission levels and Vac-U-Tron found no buyers.

Trouble with the Licensor

Back in West Hempstead, Aurora's move into large-scale cars led to legal questions involving Aurora's license agreement with Carl Robinette. As intellectual property owner of the basic Aurora HO system, Robinette had been paid royalties on every Model Motoring product made since 1960.

However, when Aurora launched its large-scale slot systems, Robinette asked to be paid the same royalty on the new products. Joe Giammarino offered to pay a smaller fee (1 to 1.5 percent). Robinette refused and filed suit. The case ultimately went to trial, turning on the question of exactly what Robinette had licensed to Aurora.

Robinette claimed to have developed the slot car concept. To investigate his assertion, the court visited a local raceway and watched cars in action. Nat Polk testified on Aurora's behalf—even bringing a 1912 Lionel racing set into the courtroom to demonstrate that the basic electric car idea was a very old one. Even more compelling was the revelation that, unknown to Derek Brand, Robinette had patented the vibrator motor in his own name. Carl Robinette lost the suit, but Aurora decided to sever all relations with Robinette and paid him in excess of $1 million to buy out his licensor status.

The Peak

1966 was the peak of the big car slot car boom. *Craft, Model and Hobby Industry* estimated that the United States had more slot raceways than bowling alleys—"over 5,000." More conservative estimates placed the number of properly equipped, full-time race centers at 600. But the dollar figures didn't exaggerate a thing: total sales of slot car equipment had risen from $100 million in 1964 to $170 million in 1965, and the growth curve was still headed toward the sky.

As slot fever soared, voices of concern rose. Aurora's regional survey found that in the East "slot centers are popping up like mad," while in California—where the craze had begun—the number was declining. "The quick-rise 'boom days' are nearing an end," Rich Palmer wrote in an August report. "Boom days for these centers lasted from six months to two years and then they began to disappear as fast as they opened up."

There were more insidious problems with large-scale slot cars. Raceways existed for the excitement of competition, but by 1966, a handful of racers in each market had refined their skills so well they won every race. A huge gap developed between most racers and an elite circle of pros. When average racers discovered they had no hope of winning, they dropped out of the sport for good.

In addition, the incessant demand for more speed led to a mad scramble among large-scale slot car manufacturers. The were obliged to keep coming up with better motors, tires, chassis, and every other racing-car part that might slice a fraction of a second off lap times. The result was proliferation of new products and rapid obsolescence of the old. Retailers found themselves bombarded with customer demands for the latest products while shelves were still filled with last month's hot items.

Worse, the typical teenage slot racer discovered that building a competitive race car was a very big drain on his allowance. Distributors and retailers were making less money because the numbers of people renting lanes were shrinking and they were regularly stuck with obsolete merchandise they couldn't move. And no one seemed to have the answer.

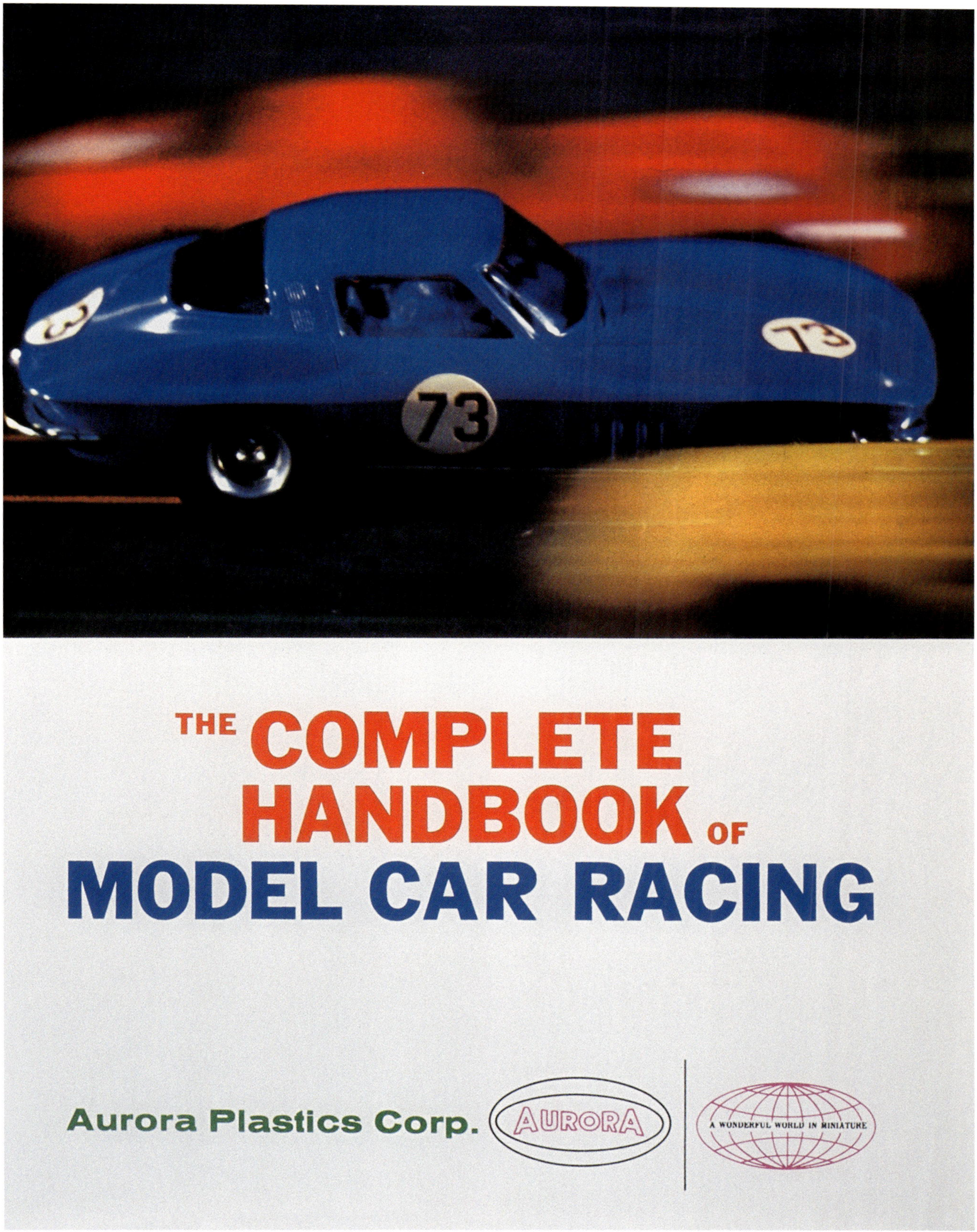

THE COMPLETE HANDBOOK OF MODEL CAR RACING

Aurora Plastics Corp.

In 1967, at the peak of the large scale slot racing boom, Prentice-Hall published Aurora's how-to book on building competition cars and track layouts.

The HO scale Thunderbike (1387 $55), Ford XL500 (1386 $60), Chevy Camaro (1388 $100), and Mercury Cougar (1389 $40).

K&B and Aurora 1/32 scale cycles. From the left are Green Machine (3357 $130), Chopper Chariot (3358 $130), and Thundercycle (3266 $200).

The HO Batmobile (1385 $190) and Black Beauty (1384 $190) cars, with preproduction test shots in alternate colors.

Aurora's Wrong Turn, K&B's Marginal Success

In this hothouse atmosphere, Aurora vowed it would become the leader in 1/32, just as it was in 1/87. The company paid little attention to the warning signs in large-scale slot car racing and forged ahead with grand development plans. For example, in 1967 Aurora brought out the innovative slot cycle, the Thundercycle (3266) to take advantage of the blossoming love affair between American boys and sporty new Japanese-made motorcycles.

Unfortunately, in the dwindling large-scale marketing environment, Aurora had chosen the wrong scale in its big-slot gamble. By the mid-1960s most serious slot racers focused on 1/24. MINRA—Aurora's clandestine race-management organization—found at its 1966 National Drag Championship that 1/24 scale cars outnumbered 1/32 by a margin of six to one. Thus in 1967 MINRA dropped 1/32 from its program. To sound the death knell, Aurora 1/32 A-Jets turned out to be a commercial failure in department stores. Nevertheless, K&B continued to enjoy reasonable success in large-scale slots. For example, K&B stole the show at HIAA 1966 with its patented Cortina Mechanical Brake. Jose Rodriguez, Jr., reported to *Car Model* (April 1966), "This Cortina mechanical brake by K&B stops like nothing I have ever seen. ... this was the only real innovation I saw at the show."

The HO scale Batmobile (1385 $190).

Traditional "brake" systems were nothing more than electrical cutoffs. The Cortina, however, was a tiny, lightweight disk brake featuring a central "drum" flanked by two Teflon disks. It fit around a car's rear axle next to the spur gear. On powered track, the brake stayed in the open position and had no effect on the car's performance. However, when current was shut off, the disks clamped together and locked up the rear axle.

With a Cortina brake in his car, a racer—particularly one with a heavy car—could retain his straightaway speed far more deeply into the curve before having to hit the brake. Suddenly skidding became a real factor in slot car racing, and it took time to master the brake. The Cortina was first sold separately as an accessory, but soon select K&B cars featured it as standard equipment.

The Blue Monster

In the race for more power, Aurora fired another salvo. Critics in the dedicated hobbyist market complained Aurora Challenger and Mabuchi motors weren't up to current performance standards. Aurora's answer—the Blue Monster. It was an attempt to free Aurora and K&B from dependence on Mabuchi. Brand later admitted, "We would probably have been better off to buy a Mabuchi, but we were stubborn."

The Blue Monster was another Brand creation, the final evolutionary development of the pancake motor. In this incarnation, the motor's appearance was radically transformed. It was shaped like a conventional can motor, with circular magnets like the Mabuchis. But instead of being fitted into a can, the Blue Monster's magnets were

K&B's Bobcat, Wildcat, and Cougar motors (top row) were made by Mabuchi; while the Challenger and Hellcat motors came from Aurora's own research and development team.

The Batmobile in large scale, courtesy K&B (1878 $600).

bound together with two metal clips. This monster had iron bearings that were spun into place with the motor secured in a wire mesh cage to protect assembly workers in case it flew apart. The Blue Monster was a very hot 3-volt motor that could turn 50,000 rpms. How would the hobby respond?

Aurora manufactured the Blue Monster in West Hempstead. K&B received a more sedate 12-volt edition called the "Hellcat" (1510). K&B marketers hyped the motor's introduction with a "Blue Monster Bonanza" in-store racing contest during the summer of 1966. Their Blue Monster (1895) ready-to-race car was advertised as one that would beat everything on wheels right out of the box. Winners would receive "K&B/Aurora Test Driver" T-shirts and be sent advance copies of new Aurora products.

When the car arrived at retail stores, hobbyists were pleasantly surprised to find Aurora's Blue Monster car a realistic McLaren I, not some hairy "thingie." It ran very well right out of the box, but—alas—was not the hoped for world-beater. No matter how hard they tried, Aurora simply could not find the silver bullet for success in large-scale slot car racing.

The Sure Hit

K&B, on the other hand, introduced its feature product of 1966: the Batmobile (1878), automotive star of the popular ABC television series and a runaway best-selling static model kit and HO slot car for Aurora. K&B made it as a ready-to-run 1/24 scale car with lots of special features: a vacuum-formed body on aluminum chassis with Cortina brake, Hellcat motor, red pinstriping, lots of chrome, and a blinking red light on top. At $14.95 it was K&B's most expensive car.

Unfortunately, it did not sell. K&B president John Brodbeck admitted it "laid an egg" because it was a poor racer—and all the Batgimmicks simply did not appeal to the serious hobbyists who populated the large scale car world.

If the Batmobile had been a success, K&B was prepared to market the Green Hornet's Black Beauty, another TV-inspired product. Aurora's K&B manager Shellie Ostrowe obtained a license agreement from 20th Century Fox, derived in part from the agreement that enabled Aurora to produce a Black Beauty model kit.

In an odd historical footnote, the Green Hornet TV show used a Black Beauty scale model during special effects sequences that was a 21" pinewood creation of Derek Brand, Andrew Yanchus, and Vic Kowalski. Aurora, it seems, was everywhere in the 1960s—even behind the scenes in Hollywood.

The PRO Experience

Despite the serious efforts by MINRA and Aurora to establish industry standards for hobbyist slot car racing, by 1966 there was still no agreement. Aurora repeatedly attempted to lead the discussion on national race standards, beginning with MINRA, but that organization ultimately had proven unsuccessful in bringing local and regional organizations together. Rival local and regional organizations sponsored by magazines and manufacturers continued to jealously defend their turf.

Aurora tried again with PRO—Model Car Racing Professional Organization. West Hempstead distributed blazer patches, window stickers, and organization literature to raceway operators and hobby dealers to bring dealers together in a national organization. There was little response.

Aurora made one last try at a national organization during the 1967 HIAA national convention. HIAA designated MINRA its national organization and set up a committee of industry leaders to lend support. But it was too late; slot racing popularity was already sliding rapidly. When Aurora withdrew its advertising from MINRA's *In the Groove* in 1967, the organization folded.

Death of a Craze

As fast as it had arisen, the slot car boom died. Its faddish character had been obvious from the start, and by 1967 the novelty had worn off. Kids tried slot cars and found them boring, too difficult to master, or too expensive.

Death did not come gradually for the large scale members of the slot car family. Nat Polk later recalled that in November of 1967 he was air shipping orders to hobby shops around the country, and then in January, 1968, he received no orders at all for large scale slot car items. Zero. Overnight the bubble had popped. Rich Palmer offered this post-mortem: "Although model car racing assumed super sales, it also became extremely expensive at the consumer level to participate continually on a daily, weekly, or monthly basis. This eventually led to its downfall, as the young people could no longer afford to stay with the hobby. Only the aficionados hung on to the bitter end, and they did not represent volume purchasing."

However, the HO segment of the slot car hobby totally escaped the carnage because it represented largely a different market—home sets purchased by average kids who enjoyed racing on a much less intense level.

Overnight Aurora found itself stuck with a large, empty raceway in West Hempstead, Long Island. Silverstein declared it "a very expensive white elephant." Aurora put it on the market, but no buyer could be found. It was ultimately closed at an enormous loss. K&B, which had managed to achieve at least moderate success in large scale, exited the slot car business in the summer of 1967.

Actually, the collapse was never complete—and commercial raceways never completely disappeared. From the heady days of 1966 when "5000 tracks" were operating, the number declined to about 1500 and stabilized. A cottage industry has continued to produce motors and accessories for die-hard, big-scale slot enthusiasts down to this day. Major manufacturers, however, never returned to the world of large-scale slot cars, and to the general public the crash of slot cars is defined by the painful year of 1967.

Racers learned that lighter weight bodies meant faster laps around the track. So K&B made a variety of clear vacuum-formed bodies for serious hobby racers.

Chapter Four
TRIALS Amid Triumphs

By July, 1966, Aurora Plastics Corporation had grown large enough to be listed on the New York Stock Exchange under the symbol "AUR." From the left: John Cuomo, exchange president Keith Funston, Abe Shikes, stock specialist Charles Schafer, and Joe Giammarino.

In July 1966 Aurora marked a corporate milestone when it joined the New York Stock Exchange. Abe Shikes, Joe Giammarino, and John Cuomo went on the trading floor with Exchange President Keith Funston to have a photograph taken holding a small Model Motoring layout.

No one enjoyed Aurora's success more than Shikes. He was an extrovert who loved to talk about his business. He once met General Motors chairman Alfred P. Sloan in a Manhattan restaurant and announced: "Last year my firm made more cars than GM!" Then he pulled out a tiny T-jet that he always carried in his pocket and proudly showed it to Sloan.

The best evidence of Aurora's slot car success was its new three-story, 148,000-square-foot facility devoted to HO Model Motoring manufacturing. It was around the corner from the old plant at 44 Cherry Valley Rd. Giammarino had supervised its construction to make sure it was configured to meet production needs of the company. To get to the new building, you walked across the roof of the old plant. Inside Aurora's now-sprawling facility workers followed yellow lines painted on the floor that designated safe walkways. Signs like "Aurora Boulevard" and "Safety Drive" marked intersections and reminded workers to avoid accidents.

Although operations in the plant were year-round, around the clock, there was a predictable cycle to production. In late December the annual catalog was published, depicting products Aurora intended to market in the upcoming year. Prototypes of new products would be shown to distributors and retailers at the HIAA show in Chicago in late January and at Toy Fair in New York in February. Orders would start to come in, and tooling would be made.

Shikes oversaw these operations in the spirit of an old-fashioned, hard-nosed entrepreneur. He distrusted fancy management plans and newfangled computers. Giammarino's operating style also was highly personalized. In his eyes no employee was a complete specialist, and Giammarino expected to give face-to-face organizational instructions when new projects were undertaken. Then everyone in the company family was expected to pull together in a team spirit. It worked.

Production manager Frank Carver recalled meeting Shikes one day in the hall and showing him some projections he had jotted down on a few sheets of paper attached to a clipboard. Shikes and Carver looked over the figures and decided then-and-there on the next quarter's output—with no board meeting, no written reports. Carver explained that the Shikes-Giammarino no-nonsense management style "made nothing but money."

This Penneys set is typical of the premium sets Aurora personalized for major customers.

Customized Sets and the Factory Environment

On the right, America's top GT racers: the Ford GT (1374 $30), Cobra GT (1375 $40), Ford J (1382 $30), and Chevrolet Chaparral (1377 $120). On the track, the foreign competition: a blue Lola GT (1378 $30) and white Porsche 906 (1376 $30). On the left: a rare brown Chevrolet Mako Shark (1380 $200), Ford Thunderbird (1383 $70), Dino Ferrari (1381 $35), and Olds Toronado (1379 $110).

As Model Motoring became the standard in the industry, "private label" sets became an increasingly profitable form of business for Aurora. Specially packaged Model Motoring sets were ordered annually in April by chain-store buyers. Sears, Montgomery Ward, and J. C. Penney were the biggest customers, but Aurora built sets for nearly fifty different retailers. Conceptualizing the sets involved members of sales, R&D, and production managers. Everyone put pencil to paper and designed sets that packed as much value as possible within price ranges set by the stores.

Summer and early fall brought a flurry of activity to West Hempstead. Boxes from packaging suppliers came in one door, were placed on the first of six assembly-line conveyor belts, and were progressively filled with track, power packs, controllers, accessories, and cars. When they reached the other end of the plant, they were boxed in cartons and loaded on delivery trucks.

Quality Control kept watch over cars as they came off the line. Each Model Motoring car had to make a short run on a section of electrified track. The handful that couldn't run or ran too slowly were sent back for rework. Cars with average performance went into sets, and those that performed above average were individually boxed and distributed to hobby shops.

The idea was to place the hottest cars into the hobby shops where slot car enthusiasts would see them, buy them, and race them, enhancing Aurora's image as off-the-shelf speed leader. (Brand and the R&D boys tried to discover why some cars ran faster than others, but they were never able to pinpoint the subtle variations that made a difference.)

Shipping was full tilt from August to December. New York retailers' trucks were still backing up to the loading dock on December 24th. January to March was another surge period, restocking the rest of the country. Then HIAA and Toy Fair, and the whole process would begin again. It was a cycle that rang cash registers across the country and filled Aurora's accounts.

What to do with the Grand National?

By 1966 the novelty had worn off the Ford-Aurora Grand National, and Aurora had to work hard to get hobby shops to participate. Aurora pledged merchandise prizes to the three shops showing the most enterprise in promoting the program. Boys wishing to race had to purchase 1967 Thunderbirds (1383) sent only to shops participating in the contest, and store winners received a chrome plated Thunderbird.

The Fifth Grand National began in the fall as Ford unveiled its new 1967 models. Aurora had been given advance drawings of the new Thunderbird so that it could unveil its car at the same time Ford displayed the real thing. Once again the semi-final competition was held at the Aurora Race Center and included races with 1/32 scale cars. Symbolic of the Grand National's decline was the fact that the final was televised only on the local New York City kids show *Wonderama*. The winner, 14-year-old Rick Hanna of Galesburg, Illinois, won a Mustang 2+2.

After a run of five years, the Ford-Aurora Grand National came to an end. It had been remarkably successful in getting thousands of store owners to add racing activities to their normal routines, and it attracted millions of boys to turn out for some very exciting races. It stands today as one of the highlights of the golden age of the neighborhood hobby shop—a time that has, alas, largely passed into history.

You Can't Fool Kids: Cigarbox

When 1967 arrived, slot cars suddenly had a new challenge to face—die-cast miniature cars. Miniature

Winner of the Fifth Grand National Rick Hanna receives his trophy from *Wonderama* host Sonny Fox and keys to a new Mustang from Aurora's Dick Schwarzchild.

Aurora's Cigarbox cars packaging clearly drew its inspiration from Matchbox's classic design.

die-casts had been around since the Tootsie Toys of the 1920s, and Matchbox had become world leader in the 1950s. Suddenly those old stalwarts, as well as Corgi, Husky, and Dinky were all the rage. Even plastic model companies joined the fray: AMT had "Pups," Lindberg brought out "Mini-Lindies," and there were others.

Never timid to join a fight, Aurora jumped in head first. Anson Isaacson, a toy industry veteran recently hired away from Ideal to advise Aurora's new games and toys division, believed Aurora could become a leader in die-cast. Isaacson, Silverstein, and Schwarzchild locked themselves in a hotel room away from the bustle of West Hempstead for an all-day brainstorming session. When they emerged from seclusion, they had come up with "Cigarbox Cars," autos individually packaged in miniature boxes with flip-top lids resembling tiny cigar boxes—clearly a derivative of Matchbox's enduring packaging theme.

Aurora had one distinct advantage: it could market dozens of cars almost immediately because of their existing slot car tooling. Competitors couldn't develop and produce variety and volume like Aurora. Create a die-cast chassis, install Thunderjet wheels and tires, and combine it with existing Thunderjet bodies and, presto!—Cigarbox. Aurora delivered its first 26 of a planned 72 cars in January and promoted the line with a beautiful Silverstein-produced TV advertisement.

Aurora invested a good deal of money to tool Cigarbox. Two lines capable of producing 30,000 cars daily were established. The only problem—a total and complete lack of demand. After the Arburg machines spewed out two weeks' worth of bodies, Cigar Box manufacture ceased. As Brand observed, kids weren't fooled—Aurora's "die-casts" were simply revamped slot bodies. Only two runs of Cigarbox cars were ever produced.

One sad result of the quick demise of Cigar Box cars was that Aurora's planned Batmobile and Green Hornet's Black Beauty cars died in the tooling stage.

Speedline: Low-Rent Lemonade from Expensive Lemons

In the midst of the miniature die-cast boom, Mattel upped the ante even more by unveiling Hot Wheels—cars with truly innovative frictionless axles that turned stogy die-casts into exciting play toys.

Faced with the Cigar Box disaster and the new challenge of Hot Wheels, Aurora changed course. Isaacson announced a new line that would rise from the ashes of Cigarbox—Speedline cars and track. The emphasis would be on play potential. Having copied Matchbox with Cigar Box, Aurora now copied Hot Wheels.

In creating Speedline, Aurora retained the die-cast Cigarbox chassis. Brand added a new slippery axle and hard-plastic wheels to roll on Aurora's Hot Wheels-derivative orange strip track. There also were several jumps, loops, and other track accessories.

Speedline sold very well in 1969 because Mattel's output couldn't keep pace with soaring demand. Bill Silverstein estimated that Aurora sold six million units in one year, a very respectable showing. But in 1970 he visited some retailers in California and found that as Mattel brought Hot Wheels production levels up, sales of Speedline stopped dead. Kids wanted the real thing: Hot Wheels. Silverstein warned Shikes that California portended what would happen in the rest of the country, but Shikes said Aurora would just have to try harder to market its product. Overriding Silverstein's warnings, Aurora continued to manufacture Speedlines—and store them in the warehouse. It would take years to sell off the inventory.

Aurora put a lot of effort into its Cigarbox City play set, but kids didn't take to the idea.

Speedline. Hot Wheels, anyone?

Yet Aurora never completely abandoned Speedline. Production later resumed at Aurora's Singapore plant. A second edition of Speedline cars on new yellow-and-orange blistercards came out in 1973, and a third edition (called Superspeedsters) was released in 1975. They were so cheap that retailers had to mark them down decisively to move them. Once again, straying from its core product line—HO Model Motoring—had proven disastrous for Aurora. And to the detriment of the West Hempstead manufacturer, the straying had only begun.

Changes in the Wind

Aurora's expensive failed venture into die-cast was part of a larger corporate agenda. By the late 1960s the company had adopted a company strategy to move into the mainstream of toys and games, a treacherous land where the profit margin potential—but also risk—was much greater.

Derek Brand played a part in setting these changes into motion. Already he had drastically altered the course of Revell with Highway Pioneers model cars and Aurora Plastics when he developed HO slot cars. This time in 1966 Brand brought drastic change when he developed a new game in his Model Motoring lab.

Because of his heritage, Brand was fond of the old English pub game skittles. In it, players knocked down wooden pins on a small platform by swinging a ball tethered to a pole anchored in the game base. Brand created a prototype and showed it first to Joe Giammarino, then to Abe Shikes and Bill Silverstein.

The concept became Skittle Bowl, a fun, hands-on diversion that would catapult to the best-selling game of 1969 and 1970. Ever wary of opportunity, Shikes believed that Skittle Bowl represented Aurora's "big break" to legitimately expand into toys. Giammarino, on the other hand, thought Skittle Bowl was a "one-in-a-million" lucky hit.

The ensuing disagreement over Skittle Bowl and its ultimate importance in Aurora's future became so profound that the original partnership—Shikes, Giammarino, and Cuomo—would break up. Long-simmering tensions among Aurora's top men finally boiled over.

The 1967–71 period became a major transitional period for Aurora. In 1967 John Cuomo escaped the harsh front-office atmosphere by retiring. A year later the company's board of directors, including Abe Shikes, forced Joe Giammarino to leave the company he had helped found. "I was fired from my own company," Giammarino declared. Then in 1969 Giammarino turned the tables on Shikes and sold his company shares to Charles M. Diker, who teamed with the rest of the company board to ease Abe Shikes into retirement.

No matter how many accessories Aurora added to Speedline cars—or new variations in packaging—youngsters just did not buy the product.

To use up its inventory of Cigarbox chassis, Aurora produced wildly-decorated vacuum-formed bodies that fit over them. To make the cars go, kids blew-up a balloon and attached it to the top of the car. The air escaped through a rubber noise maker—thus, Razzy Racers!

Charles Diker, the investor who would bring Nabisco into the world of Aurora.

After their exit from West Hempstead, the first of the old Aurora partners to pass away was popular sales manager John Cuomo, who died unexpectedly in 1971. Cuomo had been one of those unique individuals who never made an enemy and got along with everyone. Because he had been Aurora's liaison with the rest of the hobby industry, his passing was widely noted across the country.

Abe Shikes, after his ouster from Aurora, joined with several other former members of the old Aurora team to establish Addar Products Corporation in Brooklyn and continue manufacturing plastic model kits. Then Shikes retired to California where he resumed his friendship with Derek Brand. In 1987 Shikes, who had always presented the picture of robust health, succumbed to cancer. New York's hobby grandfather Nat Polk organized a memorial service in Shikes' honor.

Aurora's other founder, Joe Giammarino took his expulsion from the company very hard, but John Cuomo's widow and daughter did their best to cheer him up and encouraged him to get back into his old family skill of jewelry making as a hobby. In 1992 he passed away after a long battle with heart disease.

The New Aurora

In three whirlwind years, Aurora Plastics Corporation—at least at the top level—had become a completely different company. This transformation was symbolized by a new name for the firm: Aurora Products Corporation.

Aurora's new major shareholder and president, Charles M. Diker, was a young, cigar-smoking former vice president of cosmetics giant Revlon. He moved in New York City's highest social circles and collected contemporary art. With a Harvard Business School degree and modern attitudes, he intended to transform the company. Corporate structure changed dramatically. Indeed, it might be argued that Aurora gained a management structure for the first time. "Aurora had been run like a candy shop," explained Diker. New executives were hired, and many longtime Aurora department heads either departed or were fired. Executive offices went from bare floors to plush carpet.

Diker felt, correctly, that Aurora's former managers had done things "on the cheap," and he wanted to completely break clear of that mindset. If Aurora were to grow, it would need lots of additional capital investment. In his search for an infusion of new money, Diker hit upon food giant Nabisco, and in 1971 Aurora became a part of that corporate conglomerate.

Nabisco president Lee S. Bickmore declared "great potential" for Aurora as the West Hempstead hobby company expanded into games and toys. He wanted Aurora to increase annual sales revenues to $100 million a year. Nabisco's strategy focused on aggressive, rapid gross-sales growth to establish a dominant market position in games and toys. As the logic went, operating losses would be expected during this growth phase, but once the leadership role had been established, profits would soon follow.

As events unfolded, that's just how the strategy played out—sort of. Nabisco pumped lots of money into Aurora, and gross sales increased rapidly, but Aurora, which had never lost money, began posting sizable deficits each year. Change brought mixed results to Aurora.

President Diker felt that Aurora occupied a unique position with great untapped possibilities in both the hobby and toy markets. He wanted to vigorously lead the company into games and toys, while, at the same time, expanding its already strong position in hobbies. With the new emphasis on games and toys, Aurora's original product line, plastic model kits, slipped in importance. Model Motoring, on the other hand, continued to receive strong—indeed, increased—support. Diker felt that slot cars had growth potential in the toy market.

Powerslicks featured outrageously styled cars racing on brightly-colored flexible track.

Derek Brand was one old-timer who not only survived the bloodletting, but actually benefited. He was promoted to Vice President for Research and Development, and in 1970 introduced a product illustrating Aurora's new emphasis on toys. "Powerslicks" had been devised by Fred Addicks of Innova, a California design company. He showed it to Brand, who brought the system into production. Powerslicks' featured straight track sections that were powered, while the remainder was flexible enough to mold into banked curves.

When Powerslicks 1/32 scale cars hit the powered strips, kids pushed power buttons and the cars' momentum accelerated. The gears were engaged only while under power—so the cars were free-wheeling on the curves. Electrical power came from six D-cell batteries. Sets featured black power sections and bright orange and lavender curves. The first two cars were mod-customized "thingies" created by HMS. Later Innova added four conventional cars to the line. Unfortunately, the toy car's concept was flawed: pickup shoes dragged during the gliding phase, causing the cars to stop before they reached the powered straights. A revised second-generation design attempted to increase Powerslicks free-wheeling capabilities, but the high cost of manufacturing the system and lackluster sales doomed the line. Powerslicks lasted just two years.

State of the Union: Model Motoring

Sales of Aurora's mainline Thunderjet HO sets continued to increase in the late 1960s, even though the initial burst of enthusiasm had long since passed. HO sales hadn't been hurt by the collapse of large scale slots. Indeed, the big-slot crash probably helped Thunderjets, since it caused Aurora to channel most remaining slot car funding into HO.

As the 1960s drew to a close, Aurora began to make real improvements in Model Motoring. Perhaps most important from an operating standpoint was the evolution of the speed controller.

From the earliest days, Aurora's novel steering-wheel controller had been criticized as cute but clumsy. In 1965 it had been abandoned for a plunger-type controller with a thumb button (1347). This design was unique because it worked by compressing a stack of silicon wafers inside the plunger. The more compression, the more electrical flow through the controller—and thus increased speed. Unfortunately, the new design generated too much heat, a problem for any handheld device. As a correction, Aurora introduced the Mark II controller (1346) in 1969, but poor design caused its internal parts to stick.

To solve this problem, Aurora hired Jim Russell, president of the California slot car supply company Russkit and a leading figure in the world of big scale slot cars. He also raced Porsche Carreras on the sports car circuit and drove a Ford Cobra Daytona to work. His high-octane personality made him a good promoter. Russell was glad to join Aurora because with the crash of large-scale slots, as he explained, "my business had deteriorated to virtually nothing."

Russell's controller (1345) was based on a product his old company had marketed. Its pistol shape was innovative (the prototype had been built from a plastic toy gun), and in 1969 Aurora began including it in sets. The controller put the resistor—and its heat—into the pistol's "barrel." It also changed actuation from thumb movement to a more sensitive finger trigger. The design proved to be a permanent solution to Aurora's controller problems.

But Russell was hired for more than just his controller. Charles Diker wanted someone with serious experience in large-scale slot cars to help Aurora revive the 1/32 slot car segment. Aurora's president believed the large A-jets would be appropriate as Christmas gifts, and buyers from the big chain stores reassured him that there was great pent-up demand from the public for in-home sets. Russell, who had been through this war before, thought Diker's attempted revival was a losing proposition, but he agreed to support the project—"to my undying shame," he later confessed.

To accompany the A-jet re-launch, an all-new track system was developed by scaling up HO track with the power rails set away from the slot. The result of this costly retooling debuted in Aurora's 1970–71 Big Car Racing catalogs—but the concept never sold. "Performance was nonexistent," observed Russell. "To say the least, it was a total flop." For the record, the new A-jet set contained a Ferrari 612 and McLaren M12 (3351, 3352) and a Mirage Coupe and Ferrari 312P (3353, 3354), but only two chassis for the four bodies. In 1971 a set of "Crazy California" wheelie-trikes (3357, 3358) were added to the 1/32 line, mainly to use up existing inventory before shutting down the line.

Back in the World of HO ...

During this time Aurora continued with its Model Motoring upgrade program. In 1969 Aurora introduced an HO car that was a clear improvement on the six-year-old Thunderjet design. Called the "Wild Ones," the set included a Mustang, Ford GT, Camaro, and Cougar (1416 through 1419). Though the bodies were regular T-jets, they were molded in snow-white plastic, striped, numbered, and decorated with company logos like STP and Pennzoil.

Aurora brought back 1/32 scale cars in 1970–71. The Mirage coupe (3353 $80) on the left and the Ferrari 312P coupe (3354 $80) were Grand Prix racers, while the open cockpit McLaren M12 (3352 $70) on the left and the Ferrari 612 (3351 $70) were Can Am cars. *Cars and photo courtesy Bill Peter.*

More changes awaited under the hood. Aurora designers stuffed in a T-jet motor with hotter wound armatures, a new gear ratio, silver-plated pickups and brushes for improved conductivity, and soft sponge rubber tires. The cars were indeed "the fastest cars ever made," as the ads said, but real increases in speed were marginal.

Perhaps Aurora developed Wild Ones because it sensed a looming war with its one remaining HO competitor, Tyco. The New Jersey-based train and slot car manufacturer had been making inexpensive sets for the Christmas market throughout the 1960s, but Aurora dominated both the toy mass market and serious hobby racer sales. Tyco was perennially left with whatever remained.

In 1968, however, Tyco made news when it improved the quality of its car bodies. Hobbyists noted the changes and began speculating that Tyco was preparing for a serious run at Aurora. That speculation proved prophetic in 1970 with the launch of TycoPros. Promoted with a strong hobby advertising campaign, TycoPros featured an inexpensive Mabuchi HT-50 inline can motor crammed into a wide, low-slung pan chassis. The design allowed the motor to efficiently transmit power to the rear axle through a simple two-gear linkage. (The T-jet required five gears.) With wide racing slicks to grip the track, TycoPros were the fastest out-of-the-box cars available—except when they broke down, which was frequently, until Tyco worked the bugs out of the system.

Late-'60s slots: McLaren-Elva (1397 $35), Mangusta Mongoose (1400 $40), Dune Buggy roadster (1398 $40) and coupe (1399 $175). Also factory test shots of a silver-plated Dune Buggy body and McLaren with no paint detailing.

Evolving Model Motoring packaging, from the jewel box of the Willys Gasser (1401 $50, foreground) to the Tuff Ones' elevated display base.

Dodge Chargers in various states of decoration and assembly (1407 $240), along with the Ford Torino (1408 $190). The all-green bodies are factory test shots.

Alfa Romeo Type 33 (1409 $60) with and without chrome details, Chaparral 2F (1410 $35), Pontiac GTO in two desirable color schemes (1411 butterscotch $160, brown $110), AMX (1414 $70), and Mustang Mach I (1415 $115). Also, three factory prototype bodies that never reached store shelves.

In an effort to produce more detailed cars, HMS sculpted the AMX body pattern in acetate plastic at three times larger than HO scale.

The arrival of TycoPros threw West Hempstead's R&D staff into pandemonium. "Everybody was having a stroke," recalled Derek Brand. He considered the T-jet a better product for the home market. After all, its rugged construction represented a clear advantage to a toy manufacturer. However, when it came to the needs of serious slot car hobbyists, Brand had to admit the Tyco cars were indeed faster.

It wasn't long before Aurora's reply arrived: Tuff Ones. Part of Jim Russell's new role within Aurora was to act as the firm's "expert" spokesman to the slot car fraternity. As a result, he was a natural for introducing Tuff Ones in December 1969. Russell emphasized the Tuff Ones' new "radially oriented" magnets, which made the Thunderjet motor run faster with less heat. Tuff Ones' new soft sponge-rubber tires would "dig in" on curves. Also important, Aurora would promote the cars with ads on Saturday morning kids' TV, CBS's *Lassie*—and to hit adults who did the buying, *Championship Bowling.*

As icons of their time, Tuff Ones looked flashier than any previous Model Motoring product. Bright lemon, snow white, hot orange, lime green, and even pink and purple stripes! This was 1970, after all, and flower power was in full bloom.

This Wild Ones home race set highlights the cars' new brighter colors and paint schemes.

Of course, serious slot racers were more concerned with performance. *Car Model* ran articles on the Tuff Ones. Dale Flanagan (May 1970) judged them "sort of a 'Wild One' with hormone shots. ...more evolutionary than revolutionary." Tom Malone (December 1970) found TycoPros faster and Tuff Ones quicker on braking. This suggested that Tycos would be better on large tracks and Auroras on small, tight ones. Ed Bianchi (February 1971) thought Tuff Ones brought some long-needed improvements to the T-jet motor, but his speed tests showed "an awesome gap in performance. ...the TycoPro made mince-meat of the Tuff One in all departments." Like Malone, he thought Aurora braking power might even the competition on a real track.

Wild Ones: Wild Cougar (1419 $45), Wild Mustang 2+2 (1416 $80), Wild Ford GT (1417 $35), and Wild Camaro (1418 $80).

Lemon and yellow Flower Power Volkswagens (1404 $150, $60), Cheetah (1403 $45), Firebird (1402 $60), Formula 1 green Repco Brabham (1406 $40), Formula 1 red McLaren BRM (1405 $40).

'32 Ford pickup (1421 $130), Flamethrower McLaren Elva (1431 $45), Flamethrower Ford J (1430 $35), and a variety of Chevy El Caminos (1429 black top $120, blue $160, yellow $100). Also factory tests with nonproduction plastic colors.

Aurora had one more trick up its sleeve in 1970: HO cars with real working headlights. They were introduced at the Toy Fair in 1970 in the 24 Hours of Le Mans race set. Of course, cars that raced round the clock would need lights for nighttime driving, and Aurora's Flame Throwers had them. It was a sort of nifty idea, but kids couldn't really play with them in total darkness, so the lights didn't get much opportunity to show their stuff.

The Tuff Ones. Dino Ferrari (1481 $30), Ford GT (1472 $40), Dune Buggy coupe (1473 $35), Cheetah (1475 $35), Willys Gasser (1474 $50), Chaparral 2F (1476 $30).

On left, the three production versions of the #5 Tuff Ones AMX (1477 $35). Yellow firebird (1478 $50) and test shot red body are at top. Also shown: #21 Cougar (1479 $45), #1 production Camaro (1480 $40), and three prototype #4 bodies. Production Lola GT (1471 $65) and Volkswagen (1482 $40) with prototype bodies are at top.

Tuff Ones inspired all sorts of creative marketing, including "giveaways" of straight track sections.

Selling the Tuff Ones

Tyco or no Tyco—when it came to slot cars promotions, no one could compare to Aurora. Bill Silverstein pulled out all the stops for Tuff Ones. Aurora's new cars starred in the most extravagant slot car production ever staged for television on November 15, 1970. Silverstein had tried for years to get Aurora on Ed Sullivan's popular Sunday night TV variety show. He finally sold Sullivan on the idea of a $50,000 match race between the world's top Grand Prix drivers. CBS thought Silverstein was crazy to spend $50,000 on a toy car race, but Silverstein saw it another way—he received seven minutes of prime time exposure for his money when one minute of advertising cost $80,000.

On the eve of the Sullivan show, Aurora's Dick Schwarzchild presided over a dinner at Sardi's Restaurant in Manhattan. Four champion drivers were on hand: America's clean-cut Dan Gurney and Great Britain's heavily sideburned trio of Graham Hill, Stirling Moss, and Jackie Stewart. In the days leading up to the event each driver had honed his slot car driving skills by racing with Aurora's R&D staff. ("How many people can say they've raced against Jackie Stewart?" gushed one Aurora employee.) At the dinner there was a track set up in the corner where the stars and newsmen covering the event could race each other. Jackie Stewart admitted, "I think children can do it better than we can!"

At Saturday morning's rehearsal in Ed Sullivan Theater, Stewart's quip proved true (at least for a few seconds) as all four drivers wiped out on the first curve. During the evening's live broadcast it was Sullivan's turn to goof up, mispronouncing just about everyone's name.

The race, thankfully, was very exciting. The 32-foot track featured prototypes of Aurora's new banked curves. Each driver led at some point during the 20-lap race, but in the end Stewart prevailed over Gurney and won the $35,000 top prize. The others took home $5,000 each. In per-minute terms, it was the richest purse ever offered in a Grand Prix-style race on any scale. The only failing in the whole enterprise was that none of the Aurora people involved managed to get the "Aurora" name mentioned on air.

Scotsman Jackie Stewart accepts the champion's trophy and $35,000 from Ed Sullivan.

Aurora's real-life racers plying the slotted track: Dan Gurney, Graham Hill, Stirling Moss, and Jackie Stewart. Sportscaster Bill Mazer calls the race.

A transition set, still lacking the A/FX branding but featuring A/FX car artwork

Chapter Five
A/FX: A New Era

During the summer of 1970, Derek Brand quit Aurora. He felt cramped by Nabisco's management style—"too many meetings" took the fun out of the creative process. He also had grown homesick for California; so he returned to the West Coast, where he and his son, also named Derek, started their own toy design house.

Brand's successor as Vice President for Research and Development was Walter Moe, an Ideal Toys veteran who had worked for Aurora since 1968. Born in Germany in 1937, as a boy he had dug trenches and carried ammunition for home defense forces in the last horrific months of World War II. Now installed in the front office in West Hempstead, Moe found that he enjoyed working together with President Diker as a teammate in growing the company.

Since Nabisco was demanding that Aurora's gross sales increase drastically, they gave Moe a lot more money to fund product development. During Aurora's original partnership era, R&D had been a bare-bones operation. Moe quickly added equipment and staff to create a genuine research facility. He saw his job as one of recruiting young men—"talented, spirited fellows"—and demanding results. Moe, who spoke with a strong accent, willingly accepted the role of Prussian drillmaster. "I didn't try to win popularity contests," he later declared, although he realized the egos of his creative people had to be bolstered by rewarding achievement. Moe drove a big, black Mercedes convertible. Sometimes he and the R&D boys would pile into the "staff car," put the top down, and breeze off for lunch.

Moe described Nabisco's management philosophy as one in which various midlevel executives were thrown "into the gladiators' ring, where only the strong would survive." Departmental jurisdictions overlapped, an unavoidable reality since R&D, Engineering, Marketing, and Sales all collaborated to get a product on the shelves. Product managers (such as the head of slot cars) were several steps down the chain of command, with "lots of responsibilities and very little authority." However, product managers (with R&D under them) developed new concepts, which they pitched to the men up the corporate ladder for decisions. This upward percolation of innovation drove the product line—and the corporation.

Rethinking Slot Cars

When Derek Brand departed, Diker transferred Model Motoring leadership to Jim Keeler, the recently hired product manager of Aurora model kits. For a while he ran both lines—with two sets of headaches. Although only 30, Keeler was a well-known figure in the hobby industry; he'd steered Revell into producing super-detailed model car kits in the early 1960s. Slender with dark-rimmed glasses, Keeler looked the part of a model fanatic.

Jim Keeler was given a single job: develop a new car that would beat TycoPros yet still sell as an inexpensive mass-market toy. At the very least, Aurora needed to narrow the performance gap. This meant a car with better speed, improved handling, and enhanced body detail—not to mention easy manufacture, rugged-build quality, and low price.

The new car needed a new name. The Wild Ones and Tuff Ones names were attached to now-obsolete lines, and other suggestions—including Wipe-Outs, Muscle Machines, Street Cleaners, Super Cars, or Boss Machines—just didn't cut it. Bill Silverstein, now running an independent advertising agency, suggested that the tag "Too Hot to Handle" would be seen as a challenge by kids who'd buy the cars just to prove they could handle them. After an all-day brainstorming session, Keeler came up with his name: A/FX, derived from National Hot Rod Association's drag racing classification terms—A (hot stock sports cars) and FX for factory experimental.

The Model Motoring name would not die so easily, however. As one of the few remaining old-timers, Dick Schwarzchild argued that Aurora had too much invested in "Model Motoring" to give it up. Jim Russell also strongly opposed the name change. "I blew my stack," he later recalled. "I thought it was stupid to associate our line with the dirty T-shirt-and-leather jacket guys."

But President Diker liked the new name, so A/FX was in. As a partial compromise, "Model Motoring" continued in small letters under A/FX. The slash in A/FX would disappear in 1973.

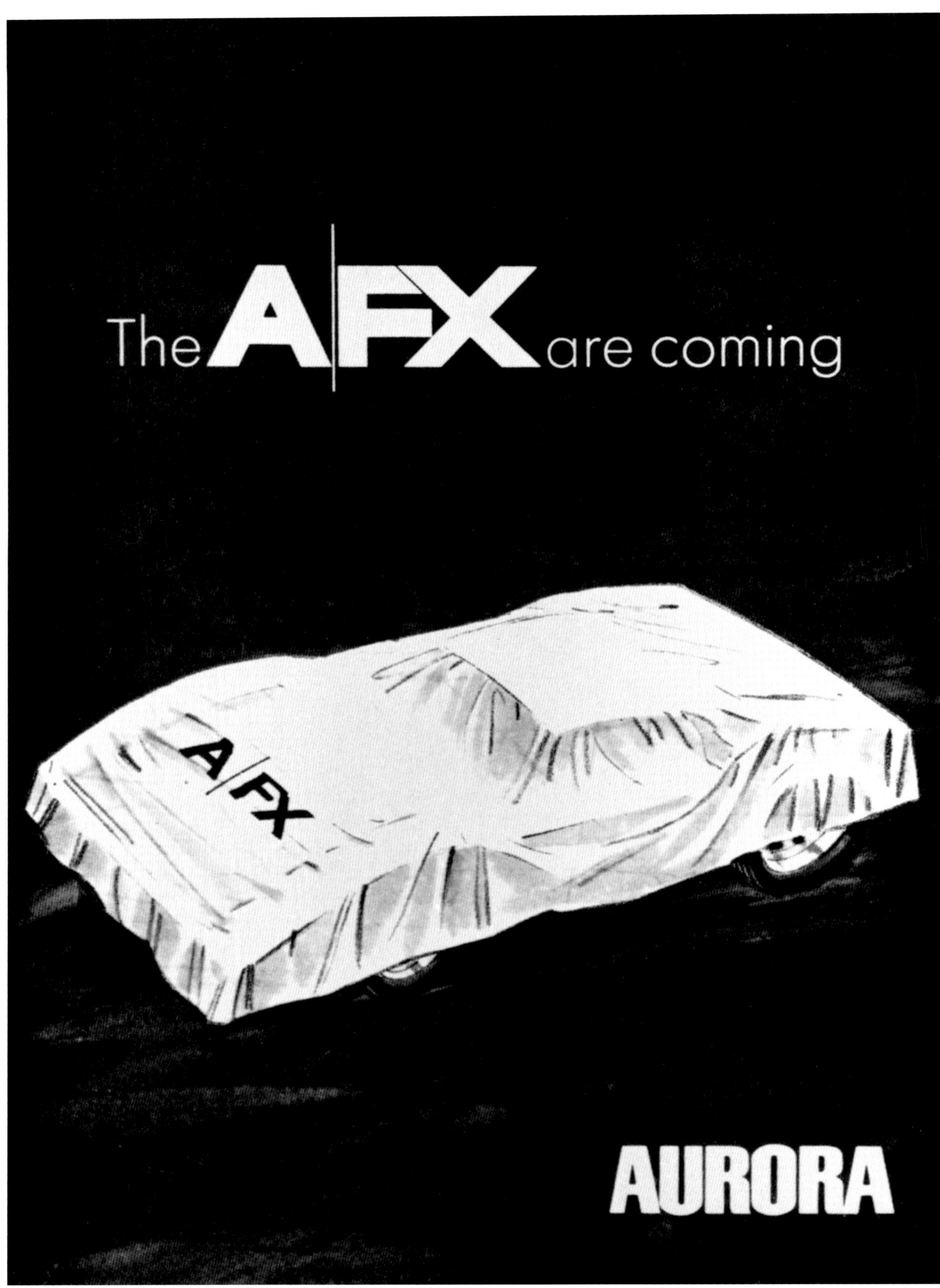

This new ad appeared in model magazines prior to release of the A/FX line to create demand for the product.

The first A/FXs: Super II (1788 $270), Grand Am funny car (1702 $100), Corvette "A" production (1703 $25), Datsun Baja pickup (1745 $25), '29 Ford Model A woody (1746 $20), Porsche 917 Can-Am (1747 $35), Dodge street van (1748 $20), #7 Auto World McLaren XLR (1752 $65), #15 Ferrari Can-Am 612 (1751 $20).

Oscar Koveleski ran the mail order catalog *Auto World* that sold model cars and slot cars. On weekends Koveleski ran a McLaren XRL painted with a slot car track running around the fenders. Aurora made it one of the first AF/Xs (1752 $25).

Innovation—Sort Of

When A/FX cars reached stores in 1971, experts raised their eyebrows. The heart of the car was still the same old pancake motor. However, evolutionary changes had been made—and they made a difference. The most visible modification was the chassis. In his last contribution before leaving Aurora, Derek Brand and chief machinist Victor Kowalski added vent holes to aid motor cooling. In addition, new axle positioning lowered the car.

Tires were wider and softer. A/FX bodies snapped on and off chassis "ears," making it easier and cheaper to assemble at the plant and also easier for kids to access the motor and gears. A new blade slot guide (as opposed to the basic pin) improved the car's track hold. Actually, the blade proved to be a hassle because you had to be sure it was pointed in the right direction to fit it into the slot. A reverse-tapered pin would follow later on and prove to be just the trick for better hold in the slot.

The A/FX bodies represented Aurora's best work. Improvements in detail were Moe's and Keeler's response to Tyco's popular new car styling. Keeler observed, "Tyco had been making tremendous inroads with K-Mart and Sears. Their individual cars were doing extremely well." As a modeler, Keeler was accustomed to intricate detail on 1/24 scale static models. He saw no reason why 1/80 scale cars couldn't be better.

In its search for better styling, Aurora's slot car division ended its long relationship with HMS's design shop that extended back to the early days of Model Motoring. HMS had fought to maintain its position, but the 1957 Chevy that it submitted as an example of its best work was deemed woefully below the standards that the new A/FX team mangers wanted.

The new producer of Aurora slot car bodies was Paramount Industries of Langhorn, Pennsylvania, whose pattern makers showed that they had a better feel for auto styling. They also sculpted their patterns in 3-to-1 or even 4-to-1 scale so that more detail could be built into the cars.

The wide variety of A/FX packaging, from Super II to late Magna-Traction

However, in order to quickly expand the initial offerings of A/FX cars, Aurora's engineering department downsized two of the HMS-designed Powerslicks bodies to HO scale. The resulting Too Much and Tubro Turnon (1754, 1755) hardly represented the kind of styling enhancement Keeler desired. "I hated 'em," Keeler declared. He thought slot cars should accurately represent real cars, not some dreamed-up "thingies." Keeler dismissed the Turboro Turnon as the "Terrible Turnoff."

The New Design Team

Moe wanted to build a whole new design team for the A/FX line. His first hire was Ron Klein, a young man from California recommended by Jim Russell, who had previously employed him to design Russkit car bodies. Blond-haired, blue-eyed, and left-handed, Klein personified the free spirit of Southern California. He also actively raced real cars in Sports Car Club of America competitions. Klein was an independent stylist who made his own design drawings and then sculpted the patterns. At first he needed some guidance from the rest of the staff on details—like making sure both sides of his patterns were symmetrical! Klein's sculpting style was described as "cartoonish," but it looked good in HO scale—perhaps more realistic than a truly accurate rendition. Klein loved European sports cars and wanted Aurora to make lots of them.

This sometimes led to clashes with Keeler, who revered American street machines and knew just which cars were hot with auto enthusiasts. The debate's legacy was a creative mix of car designs, executed in the best detail ever offered in HO.

Klein was entrusted by Keeler with Aurora sports car design, but Keeler traveled to the prestigious Art Center College for Design in Los Angeles to hire a designer for the rest of the line. Richard "Rake" Ratkiewich had hoped to go to Detroit and design 1/1 scale autos, like many Art Center grads, but instead went to West Hempstead to tackle automotive projects in smaller scale.

A year later Rake raided his alma mater for more talent. John Vernon showed that he had mastered the toy company technique of designing models from magazine photos; he became Ratkiewich's number two. In 1973, another visit to the Art Center netted Ken Hill. Thus three Art Center alums, Ratkiewich, Vernon, and Hill, became the A/FX design department for all Detroit-inspired cars. (Never slow for work, the three also styled Aurora toys and games.) Their designs would be sent to Paramount Industries (or occasionally an independent sculptor) where the patterns would be created.

Final Thunderjets: the Dune Buggy (1483 $45), Super modified roadster (1484 $170), Snowmobile (1485 $40), and Good Humor premium truck (1487 $75).

The Difficulties of Design

Chief among challenges for slot car designers was the fact that bodies had to be distorted in order to fit over the A/FX motor and onto a standard chassis with a fixed wheelbase. To make matters worse, autos differing in size—from a NASCAR stocker to a Volkswagen—had to ride the same slot car chassis. (The Vibrator and T-jet chassis had somewhat lessened this problem by offering alternate sets of holes for the front axle.) Ratkiewich made the strategic decision to design each car to fit its wheelbase, rather than match a standard scale among A/FX cars. Thus a NASCAR racer would be made to a smaller scale than a Volkswagen.

Wheels posed another dilemma. Ones that rolled well were invariably too big for the car's overall scaling, creating huge wheel wells in the tiny fenders. To the dismay of the designers, there was no simple solution for cars forced to ride on a standard A/FX chassis. A "specialty chassis" with smaller front wheels and oversized rear wheels was introduced and used on some models.

Despite these challenges, the A/FX design team created some of the best-looking slot cars of all time. Mike Meyers paid tribute to his designers' use of "incredibly creative cheating" in making their tiny car models look like the real thing.

Plastic played a big role in innovation as well. A/FX cars began to feature a new variety of plastic colors and paint schemes. "We drove Dow [Chemical] crazy" with requests for exotic plastic colors, Keeler recalled. Ratkiewich's designers created three different color and paint schemes—and three window tint shades—for each car. Some highly desirable paints, like pearl finish, could not be used because of their toxic properties—management was afraid kids would put cars in their mouths!

Keeler well remembered that the '57 Chevy model kit he designed for Revell a few years earlier had become the best selling kit in the whole industry; so he had Aurora introduce a 1957 Chevy Nomad (1760). Just as he had expected, sales of the Nomad exploded. This hot-selling car received the widest range of body and tinted window plastic combinations. "We did it in umpity different colors," said Keeler. (Not surprisingly, when Tomy AFX reissued the Nomad 20 years later in 1993, it immediately became the best-selling car in the line!)

The effort to get 1971's A/FX cars into production paralleled the rush to bring out vibrators in 1960. "We worked our tails off seven days a week," remembered Ratkiewich. The effort paid off.

"A/FX sales went through the roof," declared Keeler. "We couldn't make them fast enough." Aurora slot car revenues would triple—from $15 million in 1970 to $45 million in 1976. Overall Aurora's sales went from $29 million to $82 million. Vice President Moe observed that this "explosive growth" put Aurora on track to meet its $100 million per year sales goal.

Internal Battles and the Rise of Can-Am

A/FX success vindicated the convictions of the hobby enthusiasts on Aurora's staff. Marketing executives had argued that money spent on development of a variety of cars would be wasted. Sales, they believed, would be the same if Aurora offered only a few basic car types, track options, and accessories.

Jim Keeler argued that bringing out a continuous flow of new cars made slot racing a year-round hobby, not just a Christmas toy quickly destined for the closet. As long as Junior's track was set up, he'd be buying new cars and accessories—the real profit driver for Aurora. Keeler's argument won the day.

Among the most popular A/FX cars of the period were Aurora's Can-Am road-course racers. Carved by Ron Klein, the models evoked the thrilling vehicles raced by top drivers across early-1970s America and Canada. Aurora took the headline-making Can-Am concept and shrewdly turned it into a best-selling slot car line. The series debuted with the Ferrari 612 and *Auto World* McLaren (1751, 1752). Keeler attended the inaugural Can-Am race, took photographs of every car as it rolled off its transport trailer, and had slot versions in production six weeks later—record time for Aurora. Unfortunately, lead time would never be this good again; by the mid-1970s, Aurora would require 18 months to bring a slot car to market.

Aurora's final Can-Am racers were the RC Cola Porsche 917-10K and Porsche/Audi 510K (1747, 1786). Aurora marketers cut a deal with Sears to produce the super-hot Porsche/Audi. Jim Keeler took the first shot of the 510K to Watkins Glenn and showed it to owner Roger Penske and driver Mark Donahue. Keeler was amused when the conversation turned to whether the slot car's tiny movable rear spoiler was functional. "I wish I had a tape recording of that conversation," Keeler recalled. Interestingly, Penske's real-life Porsche proved so dominant on the Can-Am circuit that it may have contributed to the series' 1974 demise.

Emergence of the Orient

By the time the A/FX line was underway, body design and pattern making were among the few parts of the manufacturing process still remaining at West Hempstead. Most other segments of the production chain had been transferred to the Orient. When Aurora R&D finished work on the prototypes, the patterns were air-expressed to the Far East, where molds were cut, bodies were produced, and cars were assembled.

Ratkiewich demanded that first painted prototypes be sent to West Hempstead for approval before production began. His reason: Hong Kong and Singapore graphic artists tended to "orientalize" decoration schemes. Painting was done by placing a series of metal masks over the car body and spraying one color at a time with each mask.

Actually, Aurora had begun transferring production to the Orient back in 1968, when they purchased 49 percent interest in Johnson Electric of Hong Kong. This firm became Aurora's motor manufacturer, allowing West Hempstead plant managers to free up floor space for toy and game production. Then in the mid-1970s, Aurora moved most production from Hong Kong to Singapore to take advantage of tax breaks. By then the only remaining A/FX manufacture in West Hempstead was packaging.

The Far East wasn't the only region to get Aurora's slot car business. Aurora's subsidiary in Rexdale, Canada, packaged Model Motoring sets (which could be exported to British Commonwealth nations duty free). A plant in Juarez, Mexico, contributed to A/FX production by making controllers and track. Aurora had a fleet of six or eight semis continually on the road from New York to Mexico shuttling supplies and finished products back and forth. The reason for Aurora's diversification was simple: Aurora had to internationalize in order to lower labor costs and remain competitive. Al Davis, head of Aurora's international operations, estimated that manufacturing a slot car in the Far East cost only one-third of what it cost in New York. Aurora's business moves presaged the 1980s trend of overseas toy manufacture—a trend that today is an overwhelming fact of American toy making life.

Dodge Charger Daytona (1753 $40), Too Much (1754 $25), Turbo Turnon (1755 $20), Trans-Am Camaro Z28 (1756 $85), Porsche 917 (1757 $15), Plymouth Cuda funny car (1758 $40), Vega Van "Gasser" (1759 $25), and Chevy Nomad (1760 $70).

Thunderjets—End of the Line

During the first two years of A/FX, Aurora continued to list some Thunderjets in its catalog. After all, there was a huge T-jet inventory in the Aurora warehouse (Keeler: "literally mountains"), and West Hempstead had to get rid of it somehow. In fact, the large quantity of leftover T-jet chassis compelled Aurora to design four new Thunderjet bodies for distribution in the toy and novelty market.

The Super Modified Roadster (1484) was only a slight departure from the slot car mainstream. Remarkably, it used the body of the ancient Vibrator Hot Rod (1553, 1365) from the early 1960s. The "Sand Van" Dune Buggy and "Bushwhacker" Snowmobile (1483, 1485) were totally out of bounds. The Sand Vans came in a race set with orange "Baja colored" track; the Snowmobile came with snow-white track. These low-cost sets sold quickly and cleared Aurora's surplus inventory in short order.

The final Thunderjet was also the cutest: Good Humor Ice Cream Truck (1487). Aurora marketing managers cut a deal with Good Humor to produce 5,000 low-priced sets for sale as premiums. Good Humor not only paid tooling costs, they even supplied a real-life truck to copy. The R&D staff drove it around the parking lot at the West Hempstead plant, ringing the bell and trying to burn rubber—all part and parcel of standard model research.

And that was the last of the Thunderjets.

Ford "Baja Bronco" (1769 $25), Dodge Charger stock car (1773 $45), Bre-Datsun 240Z (1775 $20) and Bre-Datsun 510 Trans-Am (1776 $25), Chevy Bel Air (1777 $35), Volkswagen "Baja Bug" (1778 $25), and two screamers, the Lola T-260 Can-Am (1767 $15) and Shadow Can-Am (1768 $15).

Super II: Memoirs of a Teen Racer

By the 1970s HO slot racing had become serious business. Most survivors of the big-scale slot car crack-up in 1967-68 had shifted their interests to HO. Although competitive racing amounted to only a very small portion of the consumer market, Aurora wanted to excel in this area for the prestige winning lent to the Aurora name. When the first A/FX cars were tested by *Car Model* magazine, staff editors determined that the A/FXs could match or beat TycoPros in every department—except top speed.

The reason: superiority of the can motor over Aurora's pancake design. Of course, the motor made little difference on home tracks where speeds were slow. Most important, the slight TycoPro speed advantage meant nothing to the millions of kids who got Aurora sets for Christmas—and Aurora was still as dominant as ever when it came to mass sales.

Hardcore slot racers were a different story. The hobbyists who sent their hopped-up bombs humming down the long straightaways at commercial tracks almost always used can motors like the Mabuchis in Tyco cars. With such a motor-chassis combination, it seemed obvious that the TycoPros would dominate their Aurora counterparts. And nowhere was this more clearly demonstrated than at a summer 1971 race held at Brooklyn's Buzz-A-Rama center. Thirty-two can-motored cars were matched against just two cars with Aurora A/FX motors. However, to the amazement of everybody, one of the Aurora-powered cars easily defeated the field.

Some examples of the popular Plymouth Road Runner with Richard Petty-inspired "43" (1762 $40 to $100), Pinto funny car (1761 $25), Ferrari 512M (1763 $30), AMC Javelin Trans-Am (1764 $30), Javelin pro stocker (1765 $110), Corvette funny car (1766 $40).

The winning driver was Brooklyn high school senior Tony Porcelli. One phone call from Buzz-A-Rama to Keeler at West Hempstead, and the Aurora slot car product manager appeared to check out what was going on. Keeler bought the young man lunch and invited him to join the Aurora team (as soon as he graduated from school, of course). With Aurora's sponsorship, Porcelli continued racking up wins on the slot car circuit with his modified A/FX.

Meanwhile, West Hempstead R&D went to work on a new A/FX production car that incorporated Porcelli's innovations. It was intended to be a prestige item showcasing Aurora technology. Marketers planned to introduce the new car at the 1972 HIAA Show as the "Fastest Slot Car in the World." However this great a promotional idea lost some luster when Porcelli finished second at the year's final race.

Between races, Porcelli worked at the West Hempstead plant with the R&D team. He later recalled how much he enjoyed working with other enthusiasts. Great *esprit de corps* prevailed among the R&D staff, 18 men who labored in an exciting work atmosphere and proudly wore team blazers and lapel pins. At the back of the plant were track layouts where prototypes were tested, including a drag track where some motors met glorious smoking death in one superfast run down the strip. Another popular pastime was the "flame rally" race. Each driver would pick a car from the stock room, light the plastic body on fire with a match, and set it out around a looping course. The car that covered the greatest distance before burning to a melted mess was declared the winner.

Porcelli thought such fun made working in R&D great, but outside his department, he found too much dissension and infighting. "We butted heads regularly with engineering and marketing," he recalled. Part of the problem, in his opinion, came from company managers, who Porcelli saw as "fish out of water," with little idea of what slot cars were about down at the level of the hobbyist or ten year old.

Interestingly, Vice President Walter Moe agreed with Porcelli. He felt that hobbies and toys were distinctive industries in which normal market research just did not work. Moe believed that MBA types were much less useful than artistic, creative people with a sixth sense about what would excite kids.

In the battle between the corporate executives, engineers, and slot car nuts, Porcelli's little part of Aurora, his modified A/FX car "turned out to be a real nightmare. I did all the work on the prototypes—designing them, building them, and racing them—and turned them over to Engineering. R&D was still supposed to work with Engineering, but there was a lot of politics—a lot of friction between the two departments." The car based on Porcelli's design differed greatly from the car he had been racing. "I was disappointed how it turned out. I really was."

Peace Tank (1782 $20), Roarin' Rolls "Golden Ghost" (1781 $25), Porsche 510K Can-Am (1786 $25), Matador stock car (1787 $45), Ford Model A panel (1791 $35), Flamethrower Ferrari 512M (1799 $30) and Flamethrower Porsche 917 (1798 $25).

The fabulous Toy Fair raceway for 1972. Two levels of action showcased the performance and selection available to buyers of Aurora AFX. *Howard Johansen photo*.

The altered Porcelli design debuted at the HIAA convention as the Super II (1788). It was packaged in a velvet lined box, like a piece of jewelry. *Car Model*'s Howard Kilgore ran the prototype at the show, and his reaction was very positive: "Saying the car is a pleasure to drive is an understatement! The sensation of controlling an HO car with blinding speed and superb handling characteristics is pure enjoyment. ...The car will compare with the very best scratchbuilts when total performance is considered." Aurora slot car chief Jim Keeler labeled it "a holy terror."

The Super II resembled Tony Porcelli's prototype, but changes had been made to accommodate mass production. Lead weights were installed differently. Certain metal components were too soft. Braided copper pickups were terrific for electrical pickup but turned into a matted mess with use. Most disappointing were the rear tires. They were supposed to be wide and soft but were too narrow and too hard—thus the motor was just too much for the tires. "The armature was brutally fast," explained Porcelli, "and the tires didn't have the capability to transmit that power to the track. The car just sort of sat there and spun the tires."

The slot car community's chief criticism was the car's price—$12 compared to $4 for a regular A/FX. Some wondered if HO racing would price itself out of existence, just as 1/24 cars had. But despite its problems, the Super II kept up with the best scratchbuilts, and kids didn't have to be experts to keep it on track through the curves. Dale Flanagan of *Car Model* (October 1972) concluded, "Whether it's worth the $12 price tag is something you (and your banker) will have to decide." The Super II would last only two years, 1972-1973 in the Aurora catalog.

High Performance Track

Aurora built its most elaborate slot raceway ever for 1972's New York Toy Fair. Showcasing the Super II was a beautifully landscaped 3 x 16-foot monster of plywood, chicken wire, and plaster. The road course climbed up and around a foot-high mountain while a four-lane speedway oval with banked curves nestled in the valley below.

More than just a showcase for the Super II's speed, the layout highlighted the introduction of Aurora High Performance Track. Since the days of the vibrators, Aurora had been praised and damned for its track system—great on variety, but deficient in terms of performance. And as car speeds increased, track quality became increasingly important.

XLerators, the first slotless race cars: Ford J (2743 $20), Cougar (2781 $40), Willys (2782 $70), Vega (2746 $75), Chevy Blazer (2747 $45), #2 Ford GT (2742 $80), #1 Ferrari GTO (2741 $50), Camaro (2741 $35), Firebird (2742 $40), Chaparral 2F (2744 $20).

Aurora's answer was High Performance Track. Some changes were purely cosmetic, like eliminating the white middle-of-road line found on Aurora track since the days of Highways. Engineers added a deeper slot to accept the new blade-style guide pins. Most important was R&D team member Lou Accornero's interlocking-tab track connection system. Finally, an end of Aurora's pins and clips: assembly and disassembly was quicker and sections fit together more precisely, improving performance. 1973's Quikee-Lok tool made assembly even easier.

The most dramatic innovation of High Performance Track was banked curves—something hobbyists had requested for years. Aurora offered four different kinds: Banked S Curve (2543), shallow curves that created twisting "esses" on a straightaway; Hairpin Curve (2544), a steep-bank 6"-radius 180-degree turn; and the 9" Monza Banked Curve and 12" Daytona Banked Curve (2467, 2545), which could be used side by side to make a four-lane track.

Aurora encountered tremendous tooling and manufacturing problems with banked curves—which is why no other company had attempted the products. Indeed, the Hairpin Curve was simply too abrupt, causing cars to fly off at normal speeds. It was discontinued in 1974.

In addition to the Super II and High Performance Track, Aurora had one more 1972 innovation: the Diagnostic Center, four devices that helped the slot car hobbyist fine-tune his HO cars. The Weight Analyzer, Power Control, Dyno Tack, and the never-produced Tire Balancer (1546, 1544, 1545, 1547) weren't hits with racers like Porcelli and designers like Ratkiewich. They considered the devices too crude to be of any value, but Aurora executives insisted they go into production—and that they be inexpensive for toy market appeal. Unfortunately, nobody bought them. Serious racers knew they were useless, and kids who played with slot cars as toys didn't want them.

The 1973 launch catalog for XLerators.

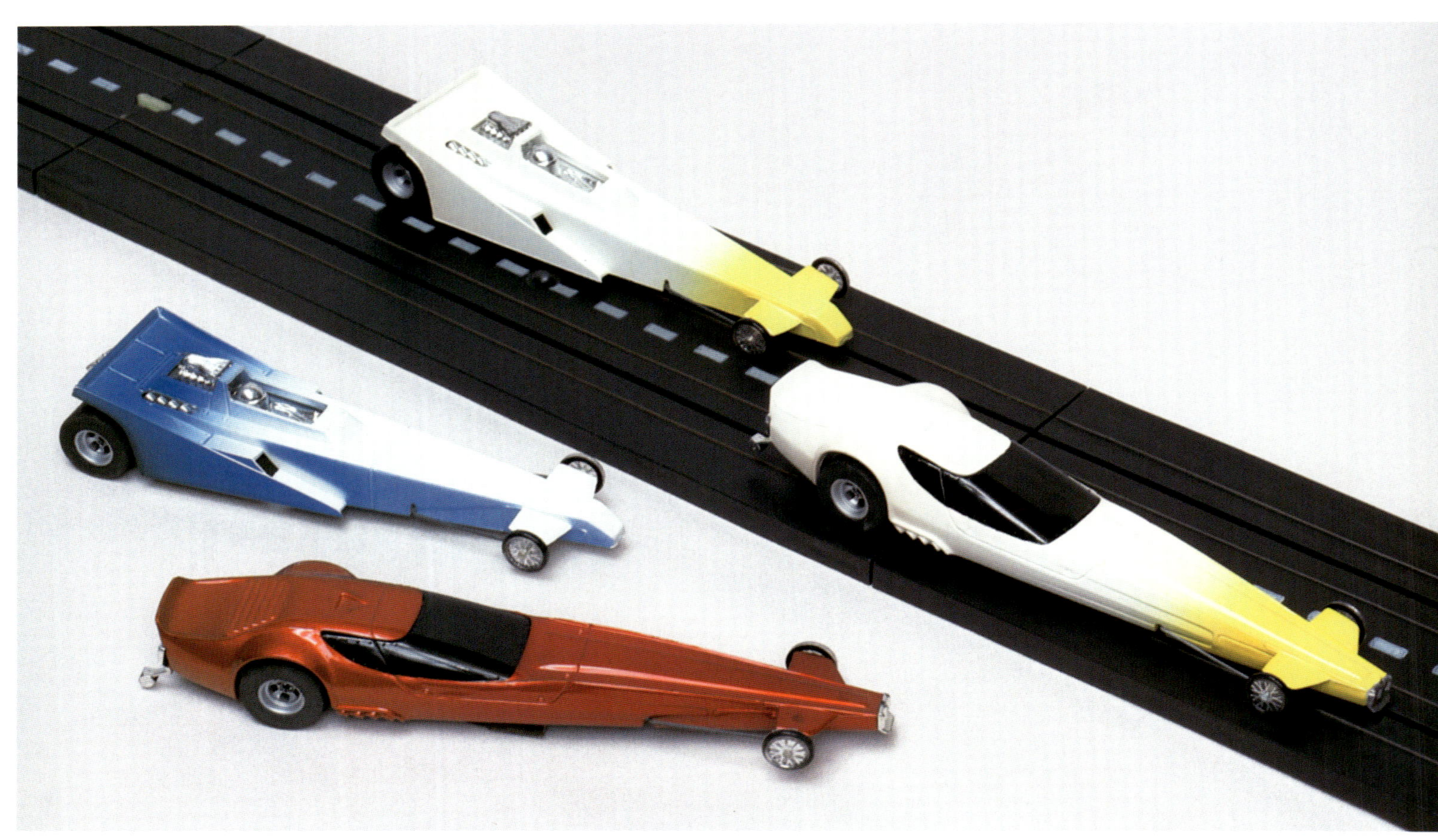

Keeler's dragsters, ungainly behemoths of the slotted road: Dyno-Mite (1794 $55), Aztec (1792 $65), Furious Fueler (1774 $50), and Dodge Fever (1772 $50).

XLerators: Innovation Never Realized

Since the days when electric slot car sets first achieved success, Aurora designers dreamed of miniature cars running free around the track, unshackled from guide pins and slots. A car that could pass on the inside lane, then move to the outside lane on a curve to gain speed would behave much more like a real race car. In the early 1970s, Aurora initiated a top-secret program in cooperation with Bell Laboratories to develop a computerized slotless system. Only Jim Keeler and a handful of Aurora executives knew about this "black" project, though it cost Aurora a serious amount of research money. Eventually the effort was abandoned because it offered no realistic hope of a low-cost product.

But innovation was out there, and it emerged from a source Aurora least expected—Montgomery Ward. The retailing giant had been offered a slotless racing concept by an independent toy designer. Ward management went to Aurora and suggested they produce the set as an exclusive for the Ward catalog. Jim Russell, who handled the Ward account, looked over the slotless racing system and pronounced it "Mickey Mouse." However, when Ward insisted they wanted it for their 100th Anniversary Catalog and would pick up initial tooling costs, Aurora went for it. Product development head Moe felt that, as industry leader, Aurora was obliged to lead the way into slotless racing.

The result was XLerators. Aurora proclaimed the arrival of "controlled racing," including authentic lane changing and passing. Aurora's R&D team did put a vast amount of work into the system's banked track and electricals, but never could get it to work properly. The idea was to create a high-speed outer lane and variable-speed inside lane between which the cars would alternate. Unfortunately, the T-jet motor lacked sufficient power to maintain speed, causing the cars to coast between power rails. Worse, the pickup shoes dragged, further slowing the car. With enough deceleration, a car could get stuck between power rails and stall. Once the cars were under way, since the front wheels were permanently fixed to a strong left turn, the only logical race strategy was to hold the throttle full open since the high outside lip of the track eliminated wipeouts.

When Aurora showed XLerators at the 1973 HIAA show, Russell installed four power packs in tandem to raise track voltage high enough to keep the cars going. "We were burning up motors right and left," he observed. Aurora, of course, had plenty of spare cars on hand to make up the losses. Would America's kids?

The appropriately named "Demolition Intersection" of 1974 gave the set its only exciting angle. XLerators II, introduced in 1976 with G-Plus motors, promised faster cars and easier setup. However, toy industry journal *Playthings* soon noted the sets' high return rates. XLerators were moderately successful as toys—but they were never taken seriously by hobbyists.

Straightaway Fever

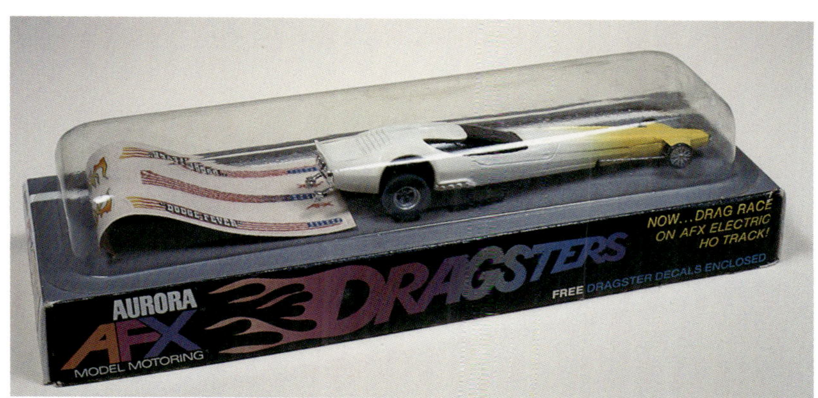

Dodge Fever (1772 $50) came in a nice display package with decals you applied yourself.

As the domain of hardcore motor-tweaking enthusiasts, miniature drag racing had been a part of the slot car scene since its early days. Derek Brand had always opposed drag racer models, feeling there wasn't enough fun in short straightaway races. However, when dragster enthusiast Jim Keeler took A/FX over, drag racers suddenly got their chance.

The result: four Dragsters (1772-1774), led by Dodge Fever, named by Keeler after his prize-winning custom model of 1968. The cars were mounted on an AFX specialty chassis, with wide slicks in the rear, a long body extension, and tiny dragster wheels out front. The Dragsters didn't sell extremely well, but Keeler remained satisfied, noting that the cars added to AFX's rising sales figures.

Aurora's 1974 AFX catalog bore the smiling face of contemporary race car driver Peter Revson, the first celebrity to serve as Aurora spokesman since Dan Gurney and Stirling Moss in 1967. Revson was a nephew of president Charles Diker's former boss at Revlon, and Diker knew Revson as a dynamic personality.

However, when Revson came to the Aurora plant at West Hempstead to discuss his role with Aurora, Dick Schwarzchild told him bluntly, "Peter, I'm sorry, but I was involved with this company when Fireball Roberts died, and I don't think [hiring you is] a smart thing to do."

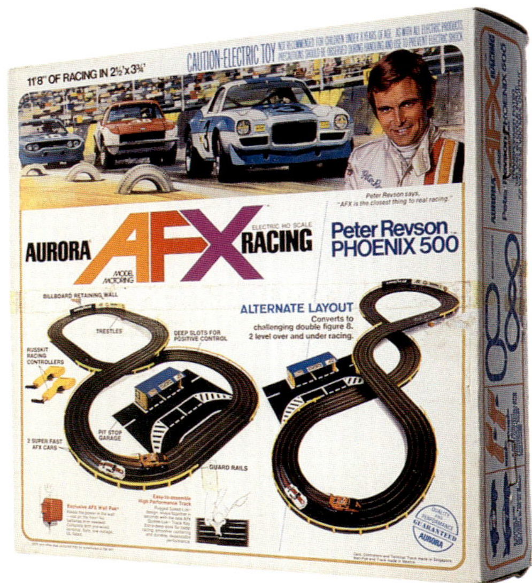

Another ill-fated Aurora celebrity spokesman, Peter Revson, whose image graces only a handful of surviving (and highly collectible) AFX packages.

Nevertheless, Revson was hired. He appeared at the HIAA convention in the Aurora suite and was a gracious, unpretentious host of the slot car exhibit. Then on March 21, shortly after Toy Fair, he was killed in a flaming wreck at the South African Grand Prix. Tens of thousands of AFX set boxes with Revson's picture were tossed into the incinerator, and labels were pasted over his picture on boxes already in the retail pipeline.

Aurora's next celebrity spokesman was Jackie Stewart—hired in 1975 only after he had retired from racing and had begun a new career as TV racing commentator. The only question about Stewart was whether his long hair might turn off parents! In 1977 Aurora would take another chance on active drivers, three-time Indy winner A. J. Foyt and six-time NASCAR legend Richard Petty.

By the 1970s, slot cars had advanced tremendously. They were faster, cornered better, and rode on superior track. But one major drawback that had been there from the beginning remained: they still sounded like tiny little electrical devices, not real cars. Back in the early '60s Rich Palmer had tried to fill the sound void by making a phonograph record called "Race-a-Rama" with the noise of real cars recorded at tracks like Watkins Glenn and Sebring. Boys were supposed to play the record while they raced their cars. The idea didn't go over.

In 1974 Aurora tried to solve the problem with "Revamatic Sound." A grandstand unit (1457) with a noise generator wired to the track made noise whenever cars were running. Aurora R&D team member Ken Hill described the sound as "scratchy," thinking it sounded like a little man under the grandstand "banging a drum." It wasn't popular at retail and wasn't around long.

On the other hand, the old track-side structure kits, first introduced in the early '60s, proved to be ad-on items with good staying power. Ratkiewich and model kit specialist Andy Yanchus got together to select new, brighter plastic colors and update the stick-on billboard labels. This time around the kits were packaged together in just two sets, rather than being sold separately.

The old slot car layout structure kits came out in the 1970s with bright new plastic colors and new racing logos. Start-Finish Pylons/Judges Stand (1498 $35) and Grand Stand/Dual Pit Stop/Curved Bleachers (1499 $70).

Get the New Year off to a Fast Start with

AURORA® AFX™

Number One in Electric Road Racing and JACKIE STEWART

World Champion Race Car Driver

Buy for shipment before the end of 1974 and save big dollars with Aurora's new special price promotions.

Jackie Stewart, newly retired from racing and unlikely to perish on a racetrack, was a natural for Aurora AFX spokesman.

Magna-Traction Flamethrowers: Porsche 917 (1973 $25), Dodge Charger Daytona (1976 $30), Ferrari 512M (1974 $30), Chevelle Stocker (1975 $25).

Chapter Six
Magnetism: Clearly Superior

AFX blistercard packaging varied with the prevailing marketing plan.

Time and pressure finally took their toll on Jim Keeler. Early in 1973 he was relieved of responsibility for Aurora's slot car division in order to concentrate on model kits. Keeler had literally worked himself into the hospital from the strain of managing two product lines.

His replacement as AFX product manager was Jim Kirby, who had once thought, "Anybody taking Keeler's job would have to be out of his mind!" Kirby began racing slot cars as a 14-year-old in Los Angeles slot parlors, and as soon as he was old enough to get his driver's license, he started racing real sports cars. He went to work for Russkit and then for hobby industry giant Revell. When R&D chief Walter Moe declared he wanted a "hot shot racer" on the staff, Jim Russell suggested Kirby. Once on board, it soon became clear that Kirby's enthusiasm and meticulous work habits made him the right choice to manage Aurora's slot car division.

Meanwhile, in the hinterlands of club racing, innovation once again rose up from the grassroots. In

Moosehead, Minnesota, a young man named Tom Bowman began winning races in 1973 with a road-hugging magnetic car that stuck to the track's metal power rails. He had simply taken three small bar magnets purchased at a craft shop and wired them to the front, middle, and rear of his car's chassis. The concept was simple but incredibly effective, eliminating the need for special brass chassis used by serious racers to lower a car's center of gravity. Bowman's discovery held any car to the road.

At a race in Indianapolis Bowman ran into Ron Esterline and John Snyder, who had independently hit upon the idea of adding magnets to the undersides of their cars. Race officials decided that these innovations constituted an unfair competitive advantage and banned the magnetic cars.

AMC Matador stock car (1930 $25), Chevelle stocker (1929 $140), 1930 Ford Model A coupe (1928 $25), VW Thing (1931 $15), Mercury Stocker (1932 $25), Porsche Carrera (1933 $20), Vega funny car (1934 $30).

Esterline looked for a way around the ban. He was an old hand at modifying the factory editions offered by Aurora and had won the Indiana state championship of the Grand National back in 1966. Esterline took an AFX chassis, cut the bottom out of the compartments that held the motor magnets, and lowered the magnets nearly to the level of the rails. The magnetic attraction of the motor magnets alone was enough to keep the car on the track.

Aurora was interested enough in what Esterline had done to send a representative out to his garage to inspect his handiwork. Allen McCall, a Midwestern enthusiast who wrote a regular column for *Car Model* magazine, shared the secret with the whole slot car world in a February 1974 article.

Purists condemned magnetism as a "gimmick." It decreased the skill demanded of drivers, they argued. Worse, magnetism heightened the already unrealistically fast scale speeds of cars to ridiculous levels. But not everyone was against change. *Car Model's* Dale Flanagan (November 1973) wrote, "Any HO manufacturer that isn't looking into this with a great deal of seriousness is missing an opportunity to make ready-to-run cars handle as well as any 'pro' HO car."

G-Plus: Ahead of the Game

What the magazine writers did not know was that Aurora was way ahead of them. In 1972, Jim Russell had been transferred to K&B's Downey, California, plant to head a new Aurora Hobbycrafts division and supervise a small team of R&D staff developing new slot car concepts. The boys in the California shop considered their place a sort of "skunk works," where new concepts could be developed without interference

Vega funny car (1934 $30), Capri funny car (1935 $30), VW Thing roadster (1936 $25), Dodge rescue vehicle (1937 $20), AMC Matador police car (1938 $30), Matador taxi, complete with quarter-panel "tire tubs" (1939 $20), 1956 Ford F-100 pickup (1941 $45), Custom Van (1942 $20), and Ford Street Van (1943 $15).

from the bureaucracy of the New York home office.

Initially, magnetic cars weren't part of the plan. Jim Russell had long felt that for Aurora to maintain its lead, they needed an efficient in-line motor/chassis unit to replace the aging pancake motor and T-jet chassis. His R&D team worked on this concept, led by chief engineer John Wessels. Jack Garcia was the machinist who built the handmade prototypes, and UCLA meteorology student Bob Bernhard provided the practical input of an active slot racer.

The three team members went to work on a lightweight racing chassis hand patterned from sheet styrene. The first prototype held a Mabuchi HT-020 motor and didn't perform well; so on the second try Bernhard replaced the Mabuchi magnets with stronger ones salvaged from an old Versitec motor. To lower the center of gravity, he reduced the gap between the chassis and track to just a paper's width. When he placed this creation on the track, to his surprise, the "killer magnets" clamped the chassis to the power rails.

The Matador Taxi (1939 $25) is a common car, but an interesting addition to collections because it bears the "Aurora" name on its side.

New AFX™ Cars with
magna traction™
An Aurora Technical Breakthrough!

Cars with Super Gripping Power—hold the track better than any other electric racing car ever!

After years of consumer frustration with slot cars that refused to stay on track, Magna-Traction was the performance innovation Aurora had been seeking.

Bernhard walked his prototype—dangling upside down from a section of Aurora track—into Russell's office. "Look at this!" he exclaimed, which produced a collective "ah ha!" from the R&D team. So arrived the basic concept for Aurora's G-Plus car.

Everyone realized a magnetic car would minimize deslotting and wipeouts—problems that frustrated kids who received Aurora sets for Christmas. Yet there remained major design issues to resolve. The prototype's magnets were so strong, they burned the motor up. Thus the problem became one of fine tuning the relationship between motor, magnets, and track. Indiana General (Aurora's magnet supplier) sent an engineer to demonstrate how stamped-metal "flux collectors" glued to the bottom of the magnets could focus the magnetism directly onto the rails. Best of all, these weaker magnets were less expensive.

The final product was a revolutionary car. Its in-line motor featured magnets and an armature held together by the plastic chassis itself. Motor magnets rested just above each power rail, and the monocoque chassis was lightweight and fast. The drive chain was a basic two-part pinion-and-crown gear linkage. In all, a racer's car suitable for mass production.

One phone call from Jim Russell was all it took to get Jim Kirby on a plane to California. He raced a Tuff Ones car against Bernhard and the G-Plus prototype. The superiority of the magnetic car was obvious. A new era in slot car racing was about to dawn.

Segmenting the Line

Despite the obvious superiority of the magnetic car, the Aurora brain trust at West Hempstead did not rush to bring it into production. AFX brand manager Jim Kirby had been running slot cars on factory tracks and doing some "blue sky" thinking about the direction of slot car development. Kirby discovered that he enjoyed racing the older—and slower—Thunderjets more than contemporary AFX cars. On weekends he was still driving full-size sports cars in rallies, and he knew that the T-jets handled more like real cars, skidding on corners and drifting on straightaways. Perhaps, he thought, Aurora's quest for ever-faster speed had taken some of the fun out of the product. Maybe a slower car had more play value, and introducing an even faster car would make slot racing even less fun.

The last of Aurora-built AFX, this time called G-Plus: mail-in premium #43 Petty Charger ($250)—not in the Aurora catalog. Also, Lola T-330 (1731 $35), #2 Ferrari 312 PB (1732 $45), McLaren F-1 (1733 $25), Ferrari F-1 (1734 $35), Indy Special (1735 $20), Ferrari Daytona coupe (1736 $25), Rallye Ford Escort (1737 $25), and Elf F1 (1738 $40).

The problem with this line of thinking, Kirby had to admit, was that "speed" sold. "The fastest car" was a concept grasped by any kid—or any buyer for a chain store.

Assistant R&D manager Mike Meyers also believed that the Aurora vs. Tyco quest for speed had become "mindless." He thought it ridiculous to pander to the top 2 percent of the market—the hardcore slot racer who bought little of Aurora's products. However, Meyers saw the real benefit of magnetism as he raced with his young son on the living room floor. Kids hated it when their cars flew off the track. A magnetic car was indeed the answer.

From his position near the top of Aurora's management, Walter Moe took a businessman's viewpoint. Moe realized the new magnetic car would render AFX obsolete, wiping out a generation of investment. He felt a go-slow, evolutionary approach toward magnetic cars would build upon the proven AFX design and be more acceptable to both Aurora's company leadership and the toy/hobby marketplace. Besides, Aurora had mountains of AFX components in its warehouses that had to be used up.

Tony Porcelli was given the unenviable task of designing a magnetic car that used as much AFX tooling as possible. His first attempt had a pancake motor flipped over to lower the center of gravity and position motor magnets as close to the rails as possible. "It was tricky," admitted Porcelli, "but it was manufacturable." Though exceptionally fast, this design would require the major retooling that Aurora wanted to avoid.

Instead, Aurora took the simpler path of installing taller magnets in the T-jet motor and lowering them in the chassis. This meant the armature was no longer centered within the magnets, but the motor still worked and, perhaps most important, represented an easy tooling modification. Aurora AFX cars with Magna-Traction were introduced as a Sears exclusive for Christmas 1974 and hit shelves nationwide in 1975.

The first G-Plus cars—based on Russell's innovative design—appeared in 1975 as well, hanging on the pegboard next to Magna-Traction AFXs. The low-end market—kids, primarily—would soldier on with the modified AFX cars, while hobbyists would support the new G-Plus design. To prevent G-Plus from stealing AFX's customers, management set the G-Plus's price at $7.50, a premium serious racers were willing to pay. After all, nothing in Tyco's stable could catch it.

The Pro View

Aurora hired pro slot racers Mike Morrissey, Nick Toma, and Jim Cawthon to conduct a series of independent tests comparing TycoPros, old AFX cars, Magna-Traction AFX cars, and G-Plus cars. Morrissey's confidential report stated, "The introduction of the new cars, particularly the G-Plus, will mark the beginning of a whole new phase of HO scale model car racing. The G-Plus is so good, it's a little eerie. The car has so much traction I still find it hard to believe. It doesn't wiggle and slide around, or even spin out, for that matter. It just digs in and goes around the track at absolutely uncanny speeds. It is faster and easier to drive than even the most sophisticated scratchbuilt cars."

Morrissey's report went on to declare that even the mainline Magna-Traction cars were "head and shoulders above old-style AFX cars. The TycoPro was the hardest to drive. Its chassis can't cope with its power." TycoPros averaged laps on Morrissey's 32-foot test track at 7.72 seconds, while standard AFXs were marginally faster at 7.57. However, Magna-Traction AFX cars blazed around the course in 6.29, and the G-Plus racers achieved an astounding 5.03 time. "It's a whole new ball game," the report concluded.

The bodies for the new G-Plus cars were Ron Klein's last contribution to Aurora—and perhaps his best. Accuracy and detail were outstanding. Indeed, the quality of the four G-Plus Formula I cars has never been surpassed by any company since. Tragically, in the midst of his most creative work, Klein's automobile crashed head-on into another car near West Hempstead. Following a prolonged hospital stay, he was homebound for months. He carved body patterns while in bed, then returned to work, but soon a stroke related to his accident made him an invalid. Klein's departure from Aurora was a true loss to the slot car world.

Nearing the End

The last sets produced by Aurora Products Corporation were unlike any others produced by the slot car pioneer. Screechers and Ultra 5 were very different products, but the sets shared more than just variants of the G-Plus motor/chassis—they were both slotless. (The basic concepts for both sets were purchased from outside design houses in California.)

Screechers Spiderman Meets the Fly, a play set for younger kids. The box shows the Spider Mobile (5811 $30) and the Fly Mobile (5812 $20).

Screechers was a fully assembled, integrated electrical and track system built into a vacuum-formed plastic base. It was a less expensive approach than conventional snap-together track layouts. Kirby felt it had a great deal of potential because two cars could run simultaneously on the same power strips and, thanks to the slotless technology, passing became a real possibility. Motor magnets (augmented by two more magnets) did a pretty good job of keeping cars on the power rails, so stalling was less of a problem than with XLerators. However, the big Screechers layout had to rest perfectly flat on the floor because any bend or twist would cause the power rails to pop out of their grooves.

Aurora marketing managers worried that Screechers might just steal the low end of the toy market from AFX sets. To avoid this, the four Screechers sets aimed to expand the market by appealing to younger children through "themes" intended to appeal to youngsters—like Spiderman Meets the Fly (5757). To play with the set all a kid had to do was install six D-cell batteries, put the cars on track, and turn the throttles.

Aurora Products Corporation's final year is symbolized by its last innovation for the elusive "serious hobbyist" market: Ultra 5, a slotless set with steerable cars. Although the West Hempstead R&D team had labored on the concept for years, it was an outside source—California R&D—that brought the concept to reality. The technology differed from that used with XLerators and Screechers. Ultra 5 eliminated troublesome banked turns and integrated three (rather than two) power rails into each lane. "A" cars ran on the inside and middle rails while "B" cars handled the middle and outside. Either car could run in either lane and, most important, either car could perform realistic passing between lanes. It was the innovation hobbyists had longed for.

Steering was the key to the magic. Ultra 5 cars featured an electromagnetic coil between the two front wheels. The racer's pistol-grip controller featured a tiny steering wheel, recalling the early Aurora controllers. Turning the wheel caused the coil to energize in one direction or another, effecting a lane change. As with

Aurora often recycled car bodies from discontinued lines into new lines. The AF/X Corvette Funny Car [illegible]766 $40) became the Screechers '76 Supervette (5786 $20).

The final AFX catalog issued by Aurora Products Corporation featured a triple-crown of racing luminaries: Stewart, Petty, and Foyt.

any innovation, there were initial problems: the coil drew lots of current and tended to overheat; it took a good bit of practice to control the cars; and most troublesome, the cars were so evenly matched, it was difficult to find the opportunity to pass! But still, Aurora had finally brought true slotless racing to market, and they did it in an evolutionary way that traced its ancestry back to the original vibrators of 1960.

The Lasting Legacy

Aurora's innovations of the 1970s continued the tradition of technological leadership that had begun in 1960. Without question Aurora, the "Big A," sold more slot cars than any other company in the world. Unfortunately, the robust condition of Aurora's slot car business did not extend to the rest of the corporation.

Aurora began to lose money in 1969. The reason: Aurora's decision to enter the game and toy market. The enormous tooling and television advertising costs simply could not be recouped—even by the high-volume sales that Aurora often enjoyed with smash-hit games like Skittle Bowl. However, many Aurora games turned out to be sales flops. Families played with them once, then put them away in the closet.

Another unexpected threat emerged in 1973-74 when the Arab oil embargo sent shock waves through the toy industry; overnight, plastic costs skyrocketed as panicky suppliers hoarded supplies. Vice President Walter Moe found himself involved in cloak-and-dagger "clandestine deals" to purchase plastic for the company. However, soon the price of plastic stabilized at a higher level, but increased costs still squeezed profit margins.

Changes in the leadership at Aurora parent Nabisco also hastened the West Hempstead firm's demise. Diker had originally courted Nabisco's buyout to gain the capital infusion necessary to underwrite Aurora's move into games and toys. Nabisco president Lee S. Bickmore supported Diker's strategy, but not long after Nabisco's takeover, Bickmore was compelled to retire because of health problems. His successors quickly grew impatient with Aurora's deficits. Overnight, they ceased the capital support and aimed for a modest profit from the scaled-back company. With these changes, Diker felt his challenge to grow the company was gone, and in 1975 he resigned.

Nabisco management retained Boyd Browne from Mattel Toys of Canada to lead Aurora's return to plastic kits and slot cars. "We're concentrating on what we do best," he announced, but it was too late. Nabisco's funding cutbacks were visible everywhere: drastic reductions in games, shrinkage of variety in model kits, and a decline in new slot car body development. Aurora had been rendered a shadow of its former self.

By 1976, many Aurora slot car innovators had left or were laid off. Walter Moe formed his own design company. Jim Keeler and Andy Yanchus, most recently in charge of model kits, were gone. Jim Kirby left early in 1977 to join Moe. Porcelli, Ratkiewich, and Vernon were laid off. When the Aurora Hobbycrafts division was closed in 1974, Jim Russell started his own business.

Ken Hill and Bob Bernhard stayed on through the end of Aurora Products Corporation and into the first years of AFX's new owners. Bernhard's name went on the G-Plus and Magna-Traction patents simply because he was still on staff when patents were applied for.

In the fall of 1976 Nabisco confirmed rumors that Aurora's various divisions were up for sale. In early 1977 Aurora model kit tooling and other assets were bought by Monogram Models of Chicago. K&B went to Leisure Dynamics and then in 1983 was sold back to its original owner John Brodbeck.

Aurora tried to reassure the hobby world that AFX was here to stay. Their advertisements reminded customers of Aurora's long, illustrious history and proudly declared AFX still #1. In fact, the general HO slot car business was so healthy that Bachman, Cox, Ideal, and Lionel had drifted back into the field to join Tyco as Aurora's competitors.

In November 1977 AFX was purchased by British toy conglomerate Dunbee-Combex-Marx. This change had the potential to strengthen the Aurora slot car product line—or diminish it. Overnight, Aurora became a division of Louis Marx & Company. In 1978 the offices at 44 Cherry Valley Road were cleaned out and locked up. Aurora assets were transferred to Marx headquarters in Stamford, Connecticut.

Some new products came out of the Stamford plant. In 1978 Magna-Sonic cars appeared, with sound that changed with the change in a car's speed. The next year saw Speed Steer, a slotless system with an uncontrolled "roadblocker" car that presented an obstacle to racers trying to pass.

Then in 1980 Aurora failed to show at the Hobby Industry Association annual convention and at the New York Toy Fair. Old timers in the hobby and toy industries were astounded by the absence of an industry stalwart. It turned out that Aurora had fallen victim to the frenzied finances Dunbee-Combex-Marx used to build its international toy empire. In February, 1980, the company filed for Chapter 11 bankruptcy. Nabisco lost most of the $7 million it was owed for Aurora.

During the summer of 1980 some investors associated with Aurora Products Canada managed to put together a deal to purchase the assets of the Aurora slot car line and business resumed in the old Rexdale warehouse and office. The most interesting new products were big-rig trucks and Speed Shifters—cars with realistic transmissions and two speeds. Clearly the emphasis was on play value and not serious hobby racing.

In 1982 Aurora Canada experienced tremendous problems with its new flex track and was not able to fill orders. Thus in 1983 another successor company went into bankruptcy.

Tomy Kogyo Ltd. of Japan picked up the Aurora/AFX trademark in 1984 and began selling a new line of cars in 1986. In that same year Coleco Industries of Connecticut went looking for a place to invest profits from its highly successful Cabbage Patch Kids. Coleco purchased Tomy's Canadian and United States divisions, including Aurora/AFX. However, just two years later, Coleco went into receivership, and Tomy resumed control of the Aurora AFX slot car line.

Today Tomy AFX sets can be found on the shelves of stores around the world.

Too Many Changes

This catastrophic tangle of events meant that Aurora AFX slot cars and sets lost their leadership role to Tyco. In a final twist of fate, many of the people responsible for Tyco's rise were the same men who had earlier contributed to Aurora's success.

In 1975 Rich Palmer tried to interest Aurora in a revival of the Grand National race series. After a visit to West Hempstead, he wrote a follow-up letter: "It was like old times meeting and working with friendly faces and interesting people." However, Aurora wasn't interested—but Tyco was. Tyco's "Curvehugger Racing Contest" started in 1978 with the same basic rules as the Ford-Aurora Grand National and Palmer even used his old "Mille Miglia" track layout—now expanded to four lanes. The series continued with modest success for several years.

Laid off by Nabisco management, Tony Porcelli found employment in Tyco R&D. He recalled an early-1980s meeting when an outside designer came in to demonstrate a new chassis design prototype. It was Derek Brand! His new 440 car could beat AFX's G-Plus. The 440's successor, the X2 (another Brand creation) raised the standards of commercial slot racers to an even higher level.

Today slot cars are a staple item in hobby shops and toy stores, but they don't enjoy the kind of market share among America's computer-addicted kids that Aurora once commanded. Enthusiasm is not lacking, however. Slot car raceways still exist, and the original generation of Aurora racers—today's adults—collect and race everything from vintage vibrators to Thunderjets and modern Tomy AFXs. The computer Internet has helped create a new community of HO slot car enthusiasts.

In fact, vintage slot cars enjoyed a kind of rebirth as the twentieth century drew to a close. In 1998 a new company, Model Motoring, Inc., revived the original Aurora trademark name, as well as the spirit of the original T-Jets. "The Thunder is Back," it declared! Soon thereafter Playing Mantis, a company that got its start reissuing copies of Aurora's old movie monster models, released Johnny Lightning "ThunderJet 500" cars. Both companies used new versions of the old Aurora bodies and the pancake motor/chassis, and both emphasized the pure skill of racing without the aid of magnetic attraction. Just like in 1961.

A really good idea endures.

Index

Price List and Photo Cross-Reference

Each car in this index is identified by its Aurora catalog number. Cars are also cross-indexed by Aurora catalog numbers for other issues of the same body. Also listed are the years the car was depicted in an Aurora catalog. **The number after the catalog listing is the page in this book on which a photograph of the car appears.** Known color variations are listed with the predominant body color listed first on any given line, followed by interior color, top color, and stripe or number color, if applicable.

Most Vibrator and Thunderjet car body patterns were sculpted by Aurora craftsmen Derek Brand, Andrew Yanchus, Lou Crisci, and Ron Kohn. Several Thunderjet bodies were created by HMS, an independent design shop in Willow Grove, Pennsylvania.

Some AFX body patterns were designed and sculpted in-house by Ron Klein. Most were designed by Aurora's R & D team, but sculpted by outside vendors, principally Paramount Industries of Langhorn, Pennsylvania. When the pattern maker or designer is known, he is identified.

Prices are estimated retail prices for cars in mint-in-the-box condition. Prices plunge for models in less-than-mint condition. Some veteran slot car collectors use a 1–10 scale. A 10 is mint in the box; 9 is mint but unpackaged; 1 is a wreck. Marketplace prices vary.

Vibrators

Vibrator bodies attach to the chassis by screw posts at the front and rear. The chassis is die-cast metal. Pickup shoes have U-shaped front ends and are not spring-loaded. The paddle-wheel gear surrounding the rear axle is clearly visible on the chassis underside.

Playcraft Vibrators

Playcraft of England sold two sets: Set 1 containing the Chevy and Ford Lorry; Set 2 containing the Jaguar and Mercedes. Set 1 sells for about $1200 and Set 2 for about $400.

3101 Jaguar XK140, 11

blue	$175
lemon	$175
red	$175
white	$175

Issued with slight changes by Aurora as 1541. The clearest difference between the Playcraft Jaguar and Mercedes and their Aurora counterparts are the thin-walled body mounting posts in the Playcraft cars. The colors of the interiors also are not standard Aurora colors. Brand-sculpted body.

3102 Mercedes 300SL, 11

blue	$150
lemon	$150
red	$150
white	$150

Issued with slight changes by Aurora as 1542. Brand-sculpted body.

3103 '58 Chevrolet Impala, 11

body/top	
blue/white	$700
green/red	$700
lemon/white	$700
red/green	$700
red/white	$700
white/blue	$700

white/lemon	$700
white/red	$700

Issued by Playcraft in England only. Seven separate body components made Aurora production unprofitable. Who wanted a '58 Chevy anyway? Brand-sculpted body.

3104 Ford Lorry, 11

cab/bed	
blue	$375
blue/white	$375
lemon	$375
lemon/white	$375
red	$375
red/white	$375
white/blue	$375
white/lemon	$375
white/red	$375

Flatbed truck without side stakes. Dual wheels on rear axle. Issued by Playcraft in England, but not by Aurora in the United States. Brand-sculpted body.

Aurora Vibrators

1541 Jaguar XK140 convertible (1960–62), 12

body/interior/boot	
black/red/tan	$45
blue/tan/black	$40
dark gray/red/black	$45
light gray/red/black	$45
green/black/tan	$45
green/tan/black	$40
lemon/red/black	$35
lemon/tan/black	$35
red/tan/black	$45
tan/red/black	$45
white/black/tan	$35
white/black/red	$35
white/red/black	$35
wine/black/tan	$60
wine/tan/black	$60

First issued with slight variations by Playcraft in England. Drivers come in a variety of shirt/cap paint color combinations; Brand gave some drivers sporty mustaches! Fold-down top comes in black, tan, red. Brand-sculpted body.

1542 Mercedes 300SL convertible (1960–62), 12

body/interior	
black/brown	$65
black/red	$65
blue/black	$50
dark gray/red	$65
light gray/red	$65
light gray/tan	$65
green/black	$50
lemon/lemon	$45
lemon/red	$45
lemon/tan	$45
red/black	$50
tan/red	$45
white/black	$45
white/red	$45
white/tan	$45
wine/black	$45

Some drivers have mustaches. First issued by Playcraft in England. Brand-sculpted body.

1543 1960 Chevrolet Corvette convertible (1960–62), 12

body/side cove/interior colors	
black/silver/red	$180
blue/silver/black	$100
blue/silver/tan	$100
dark gray/silver/black	$100
dark gray/silver/red	$100
light gray/silver/red	$100
metallic gray/silver/red	$500
green/silver/tan	$100
lemon/black/red	$100
lemon/red/red	$75
lemon/silver/red	$75
red/white/lemon	$75
red/silver/tan	$75
tan/silver/red	$75
white/black/black	$75
white/black/red	$100
white/silver/red	$75
wine/silver/black	$100
wine/silver/red	$100

Driver figure unique to this car. Brand-sculpted body. Expert vibrator collector Bob Beers believes the metallic gray car is made of standard Aurora model airplane styrene plastic.

1544 1960 Ford Thunderbird hardtop (1960–62), 12

black/tan	$155
blue/black	$75
blue/tan	$85
dark gray/black	$75
dark gray/tan	$85
light gray/black	$75
light gray/tan	$85
metallic gray/tan	$600
green/black	$75
green/tan	$80
lemon/black	$50
lemon/lemon	$75
red/black	$50
red/red	$85
red/tan	$75
tan/black	$75
tan/tan $80	
white/black	$50
white/tan	$75
wine/black	$75
wine/tan	$75

Thunderbird emblem on right rear roof post only. Brand-sculpted body. Veteran collector Bob Beers believes the metallic gray car is made of model airplane styrene.

1545 Jaguar XK140 coupe (1962), 12

body/interior/top	
black/red/black	$100
blue/tan/black	$85
blue/tan/tan	$85
dark gray/red/dark gray	$85
light gray/red/black	$85
green/tan/black	$85

green/tan/green $85
lemon/red/black $75
lemon/red/lemon $85
lemon/tan/black $85
red/tan/black $75
red/tan/red $85
tan/red/black $75
tan/red/tan $85
white/red/black $75
wine/tan/black $100
Brand-sculpted body.

1546 Mercedes 300SL coupe (1962), 12

black/red/black $125
blue/tan/black $85
dark gray/red/black $85
light gray/red/black $85
green/tan/black $85
lemon/red/black $75
lemon/red/lemon $85
red/black/black $75
red/tan/black $75
red/tan/red $85
tan/red/black $75
tan/red/tan $85
white/red/black $75
white/red/tan $85
wine/tan/black $85
Brand-sculpted body.

1547 1960 Chevrolet Corvette coupe (1962), 12

body/side/interior/top
black/silver/red/black $300
blue/silver/tan/black $100
dark gray/silver/red/black $100
dark gray/silver/black/black $100
light gray/silver/red/black $100
green/silver/tan/black $100
lemon/silver/red/black $100
lemon/silver/red/lemon $100
red/silver/tan/black $90
red/silver/tan/red $100
tan/silver/red/black $90
tan/silver/red/tan $100
white/silver/black/black $90
white/silver/red/black $90
white/silver/red/tan $100
wine/silver/black/black $90
wine/silver/tan/black $90
Brand-sculpted body.

1548 1962 Ford Galaxie Sunliner convertible (1962), 12, 13

body/interior/boot
lemon/black/white $90
lemon/red/black $90
lemon/tan/white $90
red/black/tan $90
red/tan/black $90
tan/red/black $90
tan/black/white $90
white/black/tan $90
white/red/black $90
white/tan/black $90

Brand-sculpted body. Some Sunliners have been found on a simple plastic chassis, evidently produced as static cars for model railroad layouts.

1549 1962 Ford Galaxie 500 hardtop (1962), 12, 13

body/interior/top
lemon/black/black $65
lemon/red/black $65
lemon/red/lemon $65
lemon/black/lemon $65
red/black/black $65
red/tan/black $65
red/tan/red $65
tan/black/black $55
tan/black/tan $65
tan/brown/black $65
tan/red/tan $65
white/black/black $55
white/red/black $55
Brand-sculpted body.

1550 1962 Ford Country Squire station wagon (1962), 19

body/interior/top
lemon/brown/lemon $65
lemon/red/lemon $55
lemon/red-lemon/lemon $55
lemon/tan/lemon $65
red/tan/red $65
red/tan-red/red $65
tan/red/tan $55
tan/red-tan/tan $55
white/red/black $65
white/red-white/black $65
white/red-white/red $65
white/red-white/tan $65

All have light brown/dark brown painted "wood" side panels. Some have two interior colors because only half the interior is painted. Clear top may be painted either on inside or out. Some have painted door handles and tail lights. Brand-sculpted body.

1551 1962 Ford F-100 pickup truck (1962), 19

lemon/lemon/black $75
lemon/red/black $75
red/red/black $75
red/tan/black $75
tan/red/black $75
tan/tan/black $75
white/red/black $75
white/black/white $75
Brand-sculpted body.

1552 Ford Galaxie police car (1962), 19

lemon/black/black $100
lemon/black/lemon $100
lemon/black/white
red/black/black $100
red/black/white $100
red/tan/black $100
red/tan/red $100
red/black/tan $100
tan/black/black $100

tan/black/tan	$100
tan/black/white	$100
white/black/black	$100
white/black/white	$100

Police version of Ford Galaxie (1549). There are two versions of the roof light: some editions have the light molded into the roof and painted red; other editions have a red plastic light glued on. Stars painted on sides and POLICE on trunk. Brand-sculpted body.

1553 Hot Rod roadster (1962), 19, 20
1365 (Thunderjet 500 version)

black/red	$200
blue/tan	$80
gray/red	$200
green/tan	$80
lemon/black	$75
lemon/red	$75
red/tan	$75
tan/black	$75
tan/red	$75
white/black	$75
white/red	$75

Classic '32 Ford with custom radiator "dreamed up" by sculptor Brand. The two Vibrator hot rods are the only cars with three-spoked wheel hubs. Rear tires are slightly larger than front. Vibrator has four exhaust pipes; T-jet version has only three. Decal sheet with body decorations included in box.

1554 Hot Rod coupe (1962), 19
1366 (Thunderjet 500 version)

body/interior	
black/red	$200
blue/tan	$80
gray/red	$200
green/tan	$80
lemon/red	$75
lemon/black	$75
red/tan	$75
tan/red	$75
white/black	$75
white/red	$75

'32 Ford "Deuce Coupe." The two Vibrator hot rods are the only cars with three-spoked wheel hubs. Has four exhaust pipes; T-jet version has only three. Decal sheet with body decorations in box. Brand-sculpted body.

1580 International Semi truck tractor (1962), 19

blue/black	$140
dark gray/black	$140
light gray/black	$140
green/black	$140
lemon/black	$120
red/black	$120
red/red	$300
white/black	$120
wine/black	$200

Molded-in air horn. The pattern for this truck was reworked to become the International Wrecker 1364 (Thunderjet 500 version). Brand-sculpted body.

1582 Mack dump truck (1962), 19, 20
1362 (Thunderjet 500 version)

blue	$95
dark gray	$95
light gray	$95
green	$95
lemon	$80
red	$80
tan	$80
white	$80

Beds are randomly gray or green. Vibrator body cavity has cutout section for motor; T-jet version is solid plastic. Brand-sculpted body.

1583 6-Wheel Mack stake truck (1960–62)19, 22
1363 (Thunderjet 500 version)

blue	$140
dark gray	$125
light gray	$125
green	$140
lemon	$100
red	$100
tan	$100
white	$100

Bed and Stakes come in various combinations of gray and green. Vibrator body cavity has cutout section for motor; T-jet version is solid plastic. Nine-piece body—the most of any Aurora vehicle. Brand-sculpted body.

1585 Box body trailer (1962), 19

body/frame	
gray/gray	$25
gray/green	$25
green/gray	$25
green/green	$30

1586 Van body trailer (1962), 19

body/frame	
gray/gray	$25
gray/gray/Aurora logo	$120
gray/green	$25
green/gray	$25
green/green	$25
green/green/Aurora logo	$120

Thunderjets

Thunderjet bodies attach to the chassis by screw posts at front and rear. Chassis is plastic. Pickup shoes are spring-loaded. Most T-jets came with chrome-plated bumpers, rather than the silver-painted bumpers of the Vibrators. Standard T-jet packaging is a two-piece clear box. Some came in a clear tube with yellow plastic end panels. Some were blistercarded and given stock numbers in the 1100 and 1200 range.

1351 1963 Ford Galaxie convertible (1963–69), 30

body/rugs/seats/boot	
gray/black/red/black	$150
green/black/light green/black	$150
green/light green/black/black	$150
olive green/tan/black/black	$125
olive green/tan/black/tan	$125

lemon/red/black/black $150
lemon/red/tan/red $150
red/black/tan/black $100
red/black/tan/tan $125
red/black/tan/black $100
tan/black/red/white $100
tan/brown/tan/brown $100
tan/brown/tan/white $100
tan/red/tan/tan $100
turquoise/black/white/white $125
turquoise/gray/black/black $125
white/dark blue/light blue/light blue $125
white/dark blue/white/black $100
white/light blue/dark blue/black $125
white/red/black/black $100
white/red/black/red $100
yellow/brown/tan/black $125
yellow/brown/tan/brown $125
yellow/brown/white/black $100
yellow/red/black/black $100
yellow/red/black/red $100
Brand-sculpted body.

1352 1963 Ford Galaxie hardtop (1963–69), 30

body/rugs/seats/top
gray/black/red/black $150
gray/black/red/gray $150
green/light green/black/black $150
green/light green/black/green $150
olive green/tan/black/black $125
olive green/tan/black/olive green $125
lemon/red/red/black $150
lemon/red/tan/red $150
red/black/tan/black $100
red/black/tan/red $125
red/tan/black/black $100
red/tan/black/red $125
tan/black/red/tan $125
tan/brown/tan/brown $100
tan/brown/tan/tan $125
tan/red/black/black $100
turquoise/black/gray/black $150
turquoise/gray/black/black $150
turquoise/gray/black/turquoise $150
white/black/red/red $100
white/dark blue/light blue/blue $125
white/dark blue/tan/light blue $125
white/dark blue/white/light blue $125
white/light blue/dark blue/light blue $125
white/light blue/dark blue/white $125
white/light blue/tan/dark blue $125
white/red/black/black $100
yellow/black/red/yellow $125
yellow/black/tan/black $125
yellow/brown/tan/yellow $125
yellow/brown/white/brown $125
yellow/red/black/black $100

Appears in catalog until 1969, but disappears from sales lists after 1967. Brand-sculpted body.

1353 1963 Ford Fairlane hardtop (1963–69), 30

body/interior/top
gray/black/gray $100
gray/red/black $95
gray/red/gray
green/black/black $95
green/black/green $100
green/light green/black $95
green/light green/green $100
olive green/light green/black $95
olive green/light green/olive green $95
lemon/red/black $110
lemon/red/lemon $110
red/black/red $95
red/black/black $75
red/tan/black $75
red/tan/red $95
tan/brown/brown $110
tan/brown/tan $110
tan/red/black $95
tan/red/tan $110
turquoise/black/white $95
turquoise/gray/black $95
turquoise/gray/turquoise $110
white/dark blue/light blue $110
white/brown/brown $110
white/red/black $95
yellow/brown/brown $95
yellow/brown/yellow $110
yellow/red/black $120
yellow/red/yellow $110

Appears in catalog until 1969, but disappears from sales lists after 1967. Brand-sculpted body.

1354 1963 Ford Falcon hardtop (1963–69), 30

body/interior/top
gray/black/gray $115
gray/red/black $140
green/light green/black $90
green/light green/green $125
olive green/gray/black $115
lemon/black/black $115
lemon/red/black $135
red/black/black $90
red/black/red $115
red/black/tan $90
red/tan/black $90
red/tan/red $115
tan/black/black $90
tan/black/tan $115
tan/brown/brown $90
tan/brown/tan $115
tan/red/black $90
turquoise/black/black $90
turquoise/black/white $90
turquoise/gray/black $90
white/dark blue/dark blue $135
white/dark blue/light blue $135
white/red/black $100
white/red/red $130
yellow/brown/brown $90
yellow/brown/yellow $115
yellow/red/black $90
Brand-sculpted body.

1355 1963 Ford Thunderbird convertible (1963–69), 30
1255 on blistercard.

body/rugs/seats	
slate blue/black/gray	$125
slate blue/red/black	$135
gray/red/black	$200
olive green/black/tan	$70
olive green/tan/black	$70
red/tan/black	$70
tan/brown/black	$70
tan/green/black	$70
tan/red/black	$70
turquoise/gray/black	$70
turquoise/red/black	$70
white/blue/light blue	$80
white/red/black	$70
yellow/brown/black	$70
yellow/red/black	$70

1356 1963 Chevrolet Corvette Stingray (1963–72), 30
1256 on blistercard. 1391 (CC), 6101 (CB), 6801 (SL)

blue	$70
slate blue	$120
gray	$150
green	$70
olive green	$70
red	$50
tan	$50
turquoise	$50
white	$50
yellow	$50

HMS-sculpted body.

1357 1963 Buick Riviera (1963–69), 30
1257 on blistercard. 6109 (CB), 6809 (SL)

blue	$45
slate blue	$150
cream	$45
gray	$150
green	$45
olive green	$45
red	$45
tan	$45
turquoise	$45
white	$45
yellow	$45

Aurora founder Joe Giammarino drove Buicks and was pleased when Buick finally made a hot number suitable for a slot car.

1358 Jaguar XKE coupe (1963–70), 30
1258 on blistercard. 1392 (CC)

black	$90
blue	$40
slate blue	$100
gray	$100
green	$40
olive green	$40
red	$40
tan	$40
turquoise	$40
white	$40
yellow	$40

Brand-sculpted body.

1359 Indianapolis racer (1963–70), 33
1259 on blistercard.

gray	$80
lemon	$70
olive green	$80
red	$30
tan	$30
turquoise	$30
white	$30
yellow	$30

numbers: 1, 2, 3, 5, 7, 11, 13
number field: red, white, yellow
number ball: black, red, white
number circle: black, red, white, silver
interior: black, red, wine, white, silver

Designer Brand considered the Indy racer the worst-looking body he ever made for Aurora: “It looked like a fat cigar with wheels!” Bodies were bloated to accommodate the pancake motor. Good seller.

1360 Chrome-plated Indianapolis racer (1965–69), 33

silver	$40
gold	$40

numbers: 1, 2, 3, 5, 7, 11, 13 in white
number ball: black
number circle: red

Same car as 1359. The regular car sold for $2.98; chrome plating boosted the price to $3.49. Brand-sculpted body.

1361 Grand Prix racer (1965–70), 33
1261 on blistercard. 1393 (CC)

green	$55
red	$35
tan	$35
turquoise	$35
white	$35
yellow	$35

numbers: 2, 3, 5, 6, 7

Cigar-shaped body to accept pancake motor. Model Car & Science (July 1968) called it “100% pure thingie.” Appears in 1965 catalog but not on sales lists until 1966. Brand-sculpted body.

1361 International truck trailer (1963), 33
Listed in the 1963 catalog but never produced. Pairs with the Vibrator International Semi truck tractor (1580), which could not become a T-jet because pancake motor precluded a hitch; the Semi was converted into the Tow Truck (1364).

1362 Mack dump truck (1963–72), 33
1852 (VB)

cab/bed	
green/gray	$60
olive green/gray	$75
olive green/green (would this be made?)	$75
red/gray	$60
red/green	$60
tan/gray	$60

tan/green	$60
turquoise/gray	$75
turquoise/green	$75
white/gray	$60
white/green	$60
yellow/gray	$60
yellow/green	$60

"Ford" on front. To convert from a Vibrator to T-jet made it necessary to widen the body cavity to accept the pancake motor. Cutout in Vibrator body cavity was eliminated.

1363 Mack stake truck (1963–72), 33
1583 (VB)

green	$90
olive green	$190
red	$70
tan	$70
turquoise	$190
white	$70
yellow	$70

Bed and stakes come in a variety of combinations of gray and green. Ford on front. Body cavity widened to convert from vibrator to T-jet. However, the cutout in the Vibrator body cavity was eliminated. Body has more parts than any other T-jet.

1364 International wrecker tow truck (1964–72), 33

body/side stripe	
green/black	$90
olive green/black	$90
red/black	$60
red/white	$400
tan/red	$60
turquoise/black	$300
white/red	$60
white/yellow rear/red	$300
yellow/red	$60

Converted from the Vibrator Semi truck tractor (1580). Body cavity widened to convert from a vibrator to T-jet. Has molded cab-roof light (not horn, as in Vibrator version), but a few all-red issues with horn have turned up. Brand-sculpted body.

1365 Hot Rod roadster (1964–72), 34
1265 on blistercard. 1553 (VB)

black/red	$200
blue/black	$75
gray/black	$200
green/black	$75
olive green/black	$75
olive green/light green	$75
red/black	$55
red/tan	$55
tan/black	$55
tan/dark blue	$55
tan/brown	$55
tan/red	$55
turquoise/black	$75
white/black	$55
white/red	$55
yellow/brown	$55
yellow/red	$55

To convert from a Vibrator into a T-jet the body had to be widened to accept the pancake motor. This was done by eliminating the fourth (rear) exhaust pipe on each side of the body and bulging out the body behind the front wheel well. Has wide racing slick tires in back. Decal sheet. Brand-sculpted body.

1366 Hot Rod coupe (1964–72), 34
1266 on blistercard. 1554 (VB)

black/red	$300
blue/black	$65
blue/red	$55
gray/black	$300
green/black	$65
olive green/black	$65
olive green/light green	$65
olive green/tan	$75
red/black	$55
red/tan	$55
tan/black	$55
tan/brown	$55
tan/red	$55
turquoise/black	$55
white/black	$55
white/red	$55
yellow/red	$55

To convert from Vibrator, fourth exhaust pipe eliminated and bulge added to body sides behind front wheel well. Wide racing slick tires in back. Decal sheet. Brand-sculpted body.

1367 Maserati (1964–69), 34
1267 on blistercard.

body/stripe	
blue	$40
blue/white	$50
green	$40
green/white	$50
olive green	$50
olive green/white	$50
red	$40
red/white	$40
tan	$40
tan/black	$40
turquoise	$40
turquoise/black	$40
white	$40
white/red	$40
yellow	$40
yellow/red	$40

Brand-sculpted body.

1368 Ferrari 250 GTO (1964–70), 34
1268 on blistercard. 1394 (CC), 1493 (FT), 2741 (XL), 6102 (CB), 6802 (SL)

black (painted)/white	$100
blue/white	$40
green/white	$100
olive green/white	$55
red/black	$100
red/white	$45
tan/black	$30

turquoise/black	$40
white/red	$30
yellow/red	$30

Brand-sculpted body.

1369 '39 classic Lincoln Continental (1965–69), 34

red	$60
tan	$60
turquoise	$60
white	$60
yellow	$60

Appears in 1965 catalog, but not on sales lists until 1966. HMS-sculpted body.

1370 Ford AC Cobra (1965–69), 34

body/rugs/seat	
black/red/black (painted)	$300
olive green/gray/black	$125
olive green/light green/black	$125
olive green/tan/black	$125
red/black/gray	$80
red/black/tan	$80
red/tan/black	$80
tan/black/red	$80
tan/brown/tan	$80
tan/brown/white	$80
tan/red/black	$80
turquoise/black/gray	$80
turquoise/black/red	$80
turquoise/gray/black	$80
turquoise/red/black	$80
white/black/red	$80
white/blue/light blue	$120
white/red/black	$80
yellow/black/red	$90
yellow/brown/tan	$80
yellow/green/tan	$80
yellow/red/black	$80

1371 '65 Ford Mustang convertible (1965–69), 41

1271 on blistercard. 6118 (CB), 6818 (SL)

body/rugs/seats/boot/stripe (if any)	
black (painted)/red/black/black/white	$300
blue/black/gray/black/white	$150
slate blue/red/black/black	$175
green/black/gray/black/white	$110
olive green/black/light green/black	$170
olive green/black/light green/light green	$170
olive green/black/light green/olive green	$170
olive green/black/light green/black/white	$170
red/black/tan/black	$55
red/black/tan/black/white	$55
red/black/tan/red	$60
red/tan/black/black	$55
red/tan/black/tan	$60
tan/black/red/black	$55
tan/black/red/black/black	$55
tan/black/red/brown	$60
tan/brown/tan/brown	$60
tan/brown/tan/brown/black	$55
tan/red/black/black	$55
tan/red/black/red	$60
turquoise/black/gray/black/black	$55
turquoise/black/gray/black	$55
turquoise/gray/black/black	$55
turquoise/gray/black/black/black	$55
turquoise/gray/black/turquoise	$55
white/black/red/black	$55
white/black/red/black/black	$55
white/blue/light blue/light blue	$150
white/red/black/black	$55
white/red/black/black/red	$55
white/red/black/red	$75
white/red/black/white	$65
yellow/black/red/black	$55
yellow/black/red/black/red	$55
yellow/brown/tan/brown	$75
yellow/red/black/black	$55
yellow/red/black/black/red	$55

Brand-sculpted body.

1372 '65 Ford Mustang coupe (1965–69), 41

1272 on blistercard.

black (painted)/red/black/black/white	$180
blue/black/gray/black/white	$150
slate blue/red/gray/black (not a production car)	
green/black/gray/black/white	$125
green/black/gray/green/white	$110
olive/black/gray/black/white	$125
olive green/black/light green/black	$110
olive green/black/light green/black/white	$110
olive green/black/light green/light green	$125
olive green/black/light green/olive green	$110
olive green/black/tan/ olive green	$125
red/black/tan/black	$55
red/black/tan/black/white	$55
red/black/tan/red	$70
red/black/tan/red/white	$70
red/tan/black/black	$55
red/tan/black/red	$70
red/white/black/black	$55
tan/black/red/black/black	$55
tan/black/red/black	$60
tan/black/red/brown	$60
tan/brown/tan/brown	$70
tan/brown/tan/tan	$70
tan/brown/tan/brown/black	$55
tan/red/black/black	$55
tan/red/black/tan	$60
turquoise/black/gray/black	$55
turquoise/black/gray/black/black	$55
turquoise/black/gray/turquoise/black	$60
turquoise/gray/black/black	$55
turquoise/gray/black/turquoise	$70
white/black/red/black	$55
white/black/red/white	$70
white/black/red/black/black	$55
white/dark blue/light blue/white	$100
white/blue/light blue/light blue	$100
white/red/black/black	$55
white/red/black/black/red	$60
white/red/black/white	$60
white/red/black/light blue/red	$75
yellow/black/red/black	$55
yellow/black/red/black/red	$55
yellow/black/red/yellow	$60

yellow/brown/tan/brown $60
yellow/brown/tan/yellow $75
yellow/red/black/black $55

Brand-sculpted body.

1373 '65 Ford Mustang 2+2 (1966–70), 41
1173 on blistercard. 1416 (WO), 1501 (special issue)

body/rugs/seats/top/stripe	
black (painted)/red/black/black/white	$300
blue/black/gray/blue/white	$150
green/black/gray/green/white	$150
olive green/black/gray/olive green/white	$150
red/black/tan/red/white	$50
red/tan/black/red	$50
red/tan/black/red/white	$50
red/white/black/red	$50
tan/black/red/tan/black	$50
tan/brown/tan/tan/black	$50
turquoise/black/gray/turquoise/black	$50
turquoise/gray/black/turquoise/black	$50
white/black/red/white	$50
white/black/red/white/black	$50
white/red/black/white/red	$50
yellow/black/red/yellow/red	$50
yellow/red/black/yellow/red	$50

Brand-sculpted body. Special Candy Colored Mustangs (1501) were issued for use in the Third Ford/Aurora Grand National Championship. Two cars came packaged with "tire trac" liquid, screwdriver, controller, license plate. Individual cars: $400. Complete boxed set: $1,000. Candy Colors (painted): blue, green, or red—all with silver stripes.

1374 Ford GT (1966–72), 60
1274 on blister card. 1395 (CC), 1417 (WO), 1472 (TO), 1494 (FT), 2742 (XL), 6105 (CB), 6805 (SL).

body/stripe	
black/white	$70
blue	$30
blue/black	$30
blue/white	$40
medium blue/black	$30
green/black	$30
green/white	$40
olive green/black	$40
olive green/white	$40
red/black	$30
red/white	$40
tan/black	$30
tan/brown	$30
turquoise/black	$30
white/black	$40
white/dark blue	$50
white/red	$40
yellow/black	$30

Real Ford GT-40 premiered at LeMans 1965. This slot car body appeared in more Aurora issues than any other body. Crisci-sculpted body.

1375 Cobra GT (1966–72), 60
1275 on blistercard. 1396 (CC), 6113 (CB), 6813 (SL)

black (painted)/white	$70
blue/white	$40
green/white	$40
olive green/black	$40
olive green/white	$40
red/white	$30
tan/black	$30
turquoise/black	$30
white/black	$30
white/dark blue	$40
white/red	$30
yellow/black	$30

Crisci-sculpted body.

1376 Porsche 906 (1966–70), 60
1276 on blistercard. 6112 (CB), 6812 (SL)

black (painted)/white	$70
blue/white	$40
green/white	$40
olive green/white	$40
red/white	$30
tan/black	$30
turquoise/black	$30
white/red	$30
yellow/black	$30
yellow/red	$30

Yanchus and Crisci-sculpted body.

1377 Chevrolet Chaparral (1966–72), 60
1277 on blistercard. 6114 (CB)

black (paint)	$120
blue	$50
green	$50
olive green	$50
red	$40
tan	$40
turquoise	$40
white	$40
yellow	$60
numbers: 2, 3, 5, 7	

Crisci-sculpted body. Early issues have roll bars; later do not. Roll bars add to value.

1378 Lola GT (1966–70), 60
1278 on blistercard. 1471 (TO), 6106 (CB), 6806 (SL)

body/stripe(s)	
black	$100
blue	$30
green	$30
olive green	$40
red	$30
tan	$30
turquoise	$30
white	$30
yellow	$30

Cars come with many combinations of center stripe or stripes. Crisci-sculpted body.

1379 Oldsmobile Toronado (1966–70)
6108 (CB), 60

black (painted)	$110
black	$105
blue	$70
green	$70

olive green	$70
red	$50
turquoise	$50
tan	$50
white	$50
yellow	$50

Appears in 1970 catalog, but dropped from sales lists after 1969. Crisci-sculpted body.

1380 Chevrolet Mako Shark (1967–72), 60
1280 on blistercard. 6103 (CB), 6803 (SL)

black (painted)	$90
blue	$50
brown	$200
green	$50
olive green	$60
orange	$200
red	$45
tan	$45
turquoise	$45
white	$45
yellow	$45

Later editions in brown and orange have larger wheel wells; mold had been modified to produce Flashback cars. Yanchus and Crisci-sculpted body.

1381 Dino Ferrari (1967–72), 60
1281 on blistercard. 1481 (TO), 6111 (CB), 6811 (SL)

black (painted)/white	$60
blue/white	$35
green/white	$35
olive green/white	$40
red/white	$30
tan/black	$30
turquoise/black	$30
white/red	$30
yellow/red	$30

Yanchus-sculpted body.

1382 Ford "J" (1967–72), 60
1282 on blistercard. 1430 (FT), 2743 (XL), 6104 (CB), 6804 (SL)

black/white	$50
black (painted)/white	$50
blue/black	$30
green/black	$30
olive green/black	$40
red/black	$30
tan/brown	$30
turquoise/black	$30
white/black	$30
white/blue	$30
white/butterscotch	$75
yellow/black	$30
yellow/blue	$30

Yanchus-sculpted body.

1383 '67 Ford Thunderbird coupe (1967–69), 60
1283 on blistercard. 1502 (special issue), 6110 (CB), 6810 (SL)

green	$70
red	$55
tan	$55
turquoise	$55
white	$65
yellow	$55

Chrome-plated special edition (1502, $400) was sold only in hobby shops that participated in the Fifth Ford-Aurora Grand National. Yanchus-sculpted body.

1384 Green Hornet's Black Beauty (1967–69), 54
1284 on blistercard.

black/green sticker	$190

Customized Chrysler Imperial, the only four-door T-jet. $3.49 price versus $2.98 regular Aurora price. Brand/Yanchus-sculpted body; he explained that because of its bulk, the Black Beauty was one of the few bodies that didn't have to be distorted to accept a T-jet motor.

1385 Batmobile (1967–70), 54, 55
1285 on blistercard.

black/red	$190

$3.49 price. Brand-sculpted body.

1386 '67 Ford XL 500 (1967–70), 52
1503 (special issue), 6107 (CB), 6807 (SL)

blue	$60
green	$60
red	$60
tan	$60
turquoise	$60
white	$60
yellow	$60

Yanchus-sculpted body.

1387 Thunderbike (1967–70), 52
1287 on blistercard.

bike/driver	
blue-black/blue-black	$55
blue-silver/blue-black	$55
red-black/red-black	$55
red-black/white-black	$55
red-black/yellow-black	$55
red-white/white-black	$55
red-silver/red-black	$55
red-yellow/yellow-black	$55
wine-black-silver/wine-black	$70

A Derek Brand creation. Roughly 1/48 scale bike based on a Honda. Powered by a T-jet motor mounted sideways. Stabilized by pickup shoes extending from the sides far enough to make contact with the track power rails. Performed well on straights but was top-heavy on curves. Since the driver was attached to the bike by his hands, wipeouts caused him to fly head over heels! The Thunderbike race set (1319) appeared only in the 1967 catalog, and evidently was not issued, but the individual bikes were carried through 1970. "Service Kit" (8740) included replacement body, handle bars, front fender, headlight on a blistercard.

1388 '67 Chevrolet Camaro (1968–70), 52
1418 (WO), 1480 (TO), 2741 (XL), 6115 (CB), 6815 (SL)

body/stripe	
black/white	$90

blue/black	$80
blue/white	$80
brown/gold	$150
green/black	$60
green/white	$55
lime green/green	$100
red/black	$55
tan/black	$55
turquoise/black	$55
white/black	$55
yellow/black	$55

Pattern was also used for the Pontiac Firebird (1402), just like the real GM cars. After much use, the Camaro side cam tools were damaged and replaced by Pontiac tools. Thus Camaros come with original rocker panels and less heavy Firebird panels. Kohn-sculpted body.

1389 '67 Mercury Cougar (1968–70), 52

1289 on blistercard. 1419 (WO), 1479 (TO), 2781 (XL), 6116 (CB), 6816 (SL)

black	$75
blue	$45
green	$45
red	$35
tan	$35
turquoise	$40
white	$55
yellow	$35

Kohn and Yanchus-sculpted body.

Candy-Colored Thunderjets

Between 1966 and 1969, six regular T-jet cars were issued with special metallic-colored bodies. The early issues were painted; later issues were plated. These cars sold for $3.49 when regular T-jets sold for $2.98.

1391 Candy-Colored Corvette Sting Ray (1966–69), 42

1356 (Thunderjet 500 version)

Painted: blue, green, red	$75
Plated: blue, copper, green, peach, purple, red	$50

1392 Candy-Colored Jaguar XKE (1966–69), 42

1358 (Thunderjet 500 version)

Painted: blue, green, red	$80
Plated: blue, copper, green, peach, purple, red	$45

1393 Candy-Colored Grand Prix racer (1966–69), 42

1361 (Thunderjet 500 version)

Painted: blue, green, red	$60
Plated: blue, copper, green, peach, peach, purple, red	$45

All have silver stripes and numbers: 1, 2, 3, 7.

1394 Candy-Colored Ferrari 250 GTO (1966–69), 42

1368 (Thunderjet 500 version)

Painted: blue, green, red	$60
Plated: blue, copper, green, peach, purple, red	$45

1395 Candy-Colored Ford GT (1966–69), 42

1374 (Thunderjet 500 version), 1417 (WO), 1472 (TO), 1494 (FT), 2742 (XL)

Painted: blue, green, red	$60
Plated: blue, copper, green, peach, purple, red	$45

All have silver stripes.

1396 Candy-Colored Cobra GT (1966–69), 42

1375 (Thunderjet 500 version)

Painted: blue, green, red	$60
Plated: blue, copper, green, peach, purple, red	$45

All have silver stripes.

1397 McLaren-Elva (1968–72), 21, 71

1297 on blistercard. 1431 (FT), 6117 (CB)

blue/white	$40
green/white	$35
red/white	$35
tan/white	$50
turquoise/white	$35
white/red	$35
yellow/red	$35

Yanchus-sculpted body.

1398 Dune Buggy roadster (1969–72), 21, 71

1298 on blistercard.

blue	$40
green	$40
purple	$60
red	$40
turquoise	$40
white	$40
yellow	$40

Holes filled in where canopy supports for coupe version insert. At least one car with a roll bar in those holes exists. Yanchus-sculpted body.

1399 Dune Buggy coupe (1969–72), 71

1299 on blistercard. 1473 (TO)

blue	$70
medium blue	$70
green	$45
lime green	$300
orange	$175
purple	$175
red	$45
turquoise	$40
white	$40
yellow	$40

All tops are red/white. Yanchus-sculpted body.

1400 Mangusta Mongoose (1969–72), 71

1100 on blistercard. 6120 (CB), 6820 (SL)

blue	$45
light blue	$100
butterscotch	$100
green	$45
lime green	$100
red	$40

turquoise	$40
white	$40
snow white	$40
yellow	$40

Yanchus-sculpted body.

1401 Willys "Gasser" (1969–72), 72
1101 on blistercard. 1474 (TO), 2782 (XL)

blue	$60
green	$60
red	$50
white	$50
snow white	$50
yellow	$50

Drag racing side panel decals on early issues. Yanchus-sculpted body.

1402 '68 Pontiac Firebird (1969–72), 78
1102 on blistercard. 1478 (TO), 2742 (XL)

blue	$80
green	$70
red	$60
white	$60
snow white	$60
yellow	$60

Much of the pattern used to make the mold for this car body was shared with the Camaro (1388). Kohn and Yanchus-sculpted body.

1403 Cheetah (1969–72), 78
1103 on blistercard. 1475 (TO)

blue	$45
green	$45
red	$40
white	$40
yellow	$40

Yanchus-sculpted body.

1404 Volkswagen with Flower Power (1969–72), 78
1104 on blistercard. 1482 (TO)
Decorated with flowers with either rounded or pointed petals.

blue/white pointed	$70
blue/white rounded	$70
green/white pointed	$70
green/white rounded	$70
lemon/red rounded	$150
red/white pointed	$60
red/white rounded	$60
white/green pointed	$60
white/green rounded	$60
snow white/red rounded	$150
yellow/red pointed	$60
yellow/red rounded	$60

Copied from Faller's VW.

1405 Formula I McLaren BRM (1969–72), 78
1105 on blistercard.

red #11	$40

The slim-line T-jet motor was designed to fit into the special narrow chassis of this Formula I car. It sold at $4 when T-jets were $3. Slim-line cars weren't as fast as regular T-jets, and motors ran hotter.

1406 Formula I Repco Brabham (1969–72), 78
1106 on blistercard.

green #2	$40

Slim-line motor. $4 car. The real car won the World Championship in 1966 and 1967. Yanchus-sculpted body.

1407 '68 Dodge Charger (1969–72), 73
1107 on blistercard.

Body/stripe	
black/white	$300
blue/black	$120
gray/black	$190
green/black	$120
lime green/black	$120
olive drab/black	$300
lemon/black	$140
orange/black	$240
purple/black	$240
purple/white	$240
red/black	$100
turquoise/black	$120
white/black	$100
snow white/black	$140
snow white/red	$140
yellow/black	$100

All have black tops. Aurora acquired one delivery of olive-drab plastic, which it used on this car only. HMS-sculpted body.

1408 '68 Ford Torino (1969–72), 73
1108 on blistercard.

black/gold	$190
black/white	$190
green/gold	$160
green/white	$140
red/white	$140
white/red	$140
yellow/black	$140

HMS-sculpted body.

1409 Alfa Romeo Type 33 (1969–72), 74
1109 on blistercard.

body/rollbar	
blue/blue	$60
blue/chrome	$60
green/green	$60
green/chrome	$60
red/red	$50
red/chrome	$50
tan/chrome	$100
white/white	$50
white/chrome	$50
yellow/yellow	$50
yellow/chrome	$50
tallow/chrome/white circle	$60

#31 in circle on hood and sides. $3.50 when other cars sold for $3. Race decals on the sides. Yanchus-sculpted body.

1410 Chaparral 2F (1970–72), 74
1110 on blistercard. 1476 (TO), 2744 (XL)

white/black #1	$35

HMS-sculpted body.

1411 '69 Pontiac GTO (1972), 74
1111 on blistercard.

medium blue/black	$135
brown/black	$110
brown/brown	$110
brown/brown/silver stripes	$200
butterscotch/black	$160
red/black	$110
white/black	$135
snow white/black	$110

A convertible with the top up. Appears only in 1972 catalog, but appears on sales lists in 1971–72. HMS-sculpted body.

1414 '69 American Motors AMX (1970–72), 74
1114 on blistercard.

medium blue/white	$55
lime green/black	$80
lemon/black	$70
orange/mustard	$80
white/black	$70
white/red	$55

HMS-sculpted body. Typically HMS produced patterns in exact HO scale, but this car received three-times HO treatment. Produced at a time when Aurora was trying to upgrade detail level; one of the best T-jet bodies.

1415 '69 Ford Mustang Mach I (1970–72), 74
1115 on blistercard.

blue	$115
medium blue	$135
red	$140
white	$115
yellow	$115

HMS-sculpted body.

The Wild Ones

In 1969 and 1970, four regular T-jet cars were issued in snow-white plastic with racing stripes. Special tires and a decal sheet came with each. Cars feature modifications to increase speed. $4 when regular T-jets sold for $3. Packaged in a clear box with white end caps.

1416 Wild Mustang 2 + 2 (1969–70), 77
1373 (Thunderjet 500 version)

snow white/red #7	$80

1417 Wild Ford GT (1969–70), 77
1374 (Thunderjet 500 version), 1395 (CC), 1472 (TO), 1494 (FT), 2742 (XL)

snow white/orange/ black #5	$35

1418 Wild Camaro (1969–70), 77
1388 (Thunderjet 500 version), 1479 (TO), 2741 (XL)

snow white/blue #2	$80

1419 Wild Cougar (1969–70), 77
1389 (Thunderjet 500 version), 1479 (TO), 2781 (XL)

snow white/red #3	$45

1421 '32 Ford pickup (1970–72), 79
1121 on blistercard.

medium blue	$130
lime green	$130
lemon	$120
orange	$130
red	$130

Body copied from a Lindberg "Mini Lindy" model kit. Slim-line T-jet chassis/motor. $4 when other cars sold for $3.50.

1429 Chevrolet El Camino (1970–72), 79
1129 on blistercard.

blue	$160
red	$110
turquoise	$110
white	$110
yellow	$100
yellow/black top	$120

Surfboards in turquoise, white, yellow. HMS-sculpted body.

1483 "Sand Van" Dune Buggy (1971–72), 89
1183 on blistercard. 1496 (FT)

blue/white	$45
lime green/white	$35
orange/white	$45
pink/white	$35

Ratkiewich's first project at Aurora was to design a simple part to add to the Dune Buggy roadster (1398) so it could go into a low-cost toy set.

1484 Super modified roadster (1971–72), 89
1184 on blistercard. 1553 (VB), 1365 (Thunderjet 500 version)

medium blue	$170
bright yellow	$170
bright orange	$170

Spoiler and side pipes were added to the old Hot Rod roadster, resulting in this dirt-track racer. Fat sponge rear tires.

1485 "Bushwhacker" Snowmobile (1971–72), 89
1185 on blistercard.

body/driver	
blue/blue	$40
blue/lemon	$40
medium blue/lemon	$40
blue/butterscotch	$40
butterscotch/blue	$40
butterscotch/lemon	$40
lemon/medium blue	$40
lemon/lemon	$40
white/blue	$55

Simple mold designed by Ratkiewich for low-cost toy set.

1487 Good Humor ice cream truck (1972), 89

white/Good Humor labels	$65
white/Good Humor & Wild Huckleberry labels	$75

Last of the Thunderjets. Came with set of stick-on labels. Klein-sculpted body.

Thunderjet Flamethrowers

In 1970 Aurora introduced cars with headlights and tail lights to enhance their appeal as toys. They were marketed with the "24 Hours of Le Mans" (1323) race set, which attempted a realistic portrayal of nighttime driving. The "Flamethrowers" cost $4 compared to $3 for regular T-jets. Individual cars sold in a special box with white plastic base and clear, rounded top.

1430 Flamethrower Ford "J" (1970–72), 79
1130 on blistercard. 1382 (Thunderjet 500 version), 2743 (XL)

white/blue	$35

1431 Flamethrower McLaren Elva (1970–72), 79
1131 on blistercard. 1397 (Thunderjet 500 version)

black/white	$30
blue/white	$45
green/white	$45
red/white	$40

1491 Flamethrower Chaparral 2F (1971–72)
1191 on blistercard. 1410 (Thunderjet 500 version)

white/black	$35
snow white/black #7	$30
snow white/blue #7	$35
snow white #1	$30

1493 Flamethrower Ferrari (1971–72)
1193 on blistercard. 1368 (Thunderjet 500 version), 2741 (XL)

medium blue/white	$40
red/white	$50

1494 Flamethrower Ford GT (1971–72)
1194 on blistercard. 1374 (Thunderjet 500 version), 1395 (CC), 1417 (WO), 1472 (TO), 2742 (XL)

light blue	$30
light blue/black	$30
light blue/orange/black #5	$40
brown/white	$50

1495 Flamethrower Cobra GT (1971–72)
1195 on blistercard. 1374 (Thunderjet 500 version)

blue/white	$30
orange/white	$300

1496 Flamethrower "Sand Van" Dune Buggy (1971–72)
1196 on blistercard. 1483 (Thunderjet 500 version)

lime green/green	$35
pink/purple	$35

Tuff Ones

Aurora introduced the Tuff Ones in 1970—regular T-jet bodies with improvements to the motor, chassis, and tires. Bodies have new, brighter plastic colors and more elaborate body detail painting. They come in distinctive boxes with a white base and clear plastic dome.

1471 Tuff Ones Lola GT (1970–72), 81
1378 (Thunderjet 500 version)

black	$100
black/pink/white-black #3	$30
lemon/pink/white-black #3	$45
dark yellow/pink/white-black #3	$65

1472 Tuff Ones Ford GT (1970–72), 80
1374 (Thunderjet 500 version), 1395 (CC), 1417 (WO), 1494 (FT), 2742 (XL)

blue/black	$30
light blue	$90
light blue/orange-black #5	$40

1473 Tuff Ones Dune Buggy coupe (1970–72), 80
1399 (Thunderjet 500 version)

lemon/blue-white	$35
lemon/blue-white/no top (came in free track package with 1479)	$90

1474 Tuff Ones Willys "Gasser" (1970–72), 80
1401 (Thunderjet 500 version), 2782 (XL)

lemon/purple	$50

1475 Tuff Ones Cheetah (1970–72), 80
1403 (Thunderjet 500 version)

orange #2	$35
orange/no number (came in free track package with 1481)	$90

1476 Tuff Ones Chaparral 2F (1970–72), 80
1410 (Thunderjet 500 version)

lime green/blue #7	$35
white/no number (came in free track package with 1482)	$90
white/black #7	$30
white/blue #7	$30

1477 Tuff Ones AMX (1971–72), 81
1414 (Thunderjet 500 version)

red/white-blue #5	$35
red/silver #5	$25
white/blue #5	$25

1478 Tuff Ones Firebird (1971–72), 81
1402 (Thunderjet 500 version), 2742 (XL)

dark yellow/black	$40
dark yellow/black #7	$40
light yellow/black	$40
light yellow/black #7	$50
red/white painted bumpers	$35
snow white	$40
snow white/red	$40
snow white/red #7/painted bumpers	$40
snow white/red #7/plated bumpers	$40

Dark yellow and light yellow versions may be unplanned variations from the molding process.

1479 Tuff Ones Cougar (1971–72), 81
1389 (Thunderjet 500 version), 1419 (WO), 2781 (XL)

snow white/butterscotch #21	$45

1480 Tuff Ones Camaro (1971–72), 81
1388 (Thunderjet 500 version), 1418 (WO), 2741 (XL)

blue/yellow #1	$40

1481 Tuff Ones Dino Ferrari (1971–72), 80
1381 (Thunderjet 500 version)

red/green/white #3	$30

1482 Tuff Ones Volkswagen (1971–72), 81
1404 (Thunderjet 500 version),

orange/white/black #2/yellow-tinted windows	$40
orange/white/black #2/green-tinted windows	$40

AFX Super II

In 1972 and 1973 Aurora offered an HO slot car which incorporated all the hop-up techniques used by pro slot racers. The body is vacuum-formed and attaches to the chassis front with pins. Long lead weights are slung under the nose and along chassis sides. 1972 issues have braided pickups; 1973 have regular pickup shoes.

1788-880 Super II (1972–73)

red-orange #4	$270

1788-881 Super II (1973), 87

mustard #4	$270

The following two versions were announced, but evidently were not issued.

1788-882 Super II (1973)
blue #1

1788-883 Super II (1973)
white/red stripes #3

AFX

The first AFX cars were introduced in 1971. Some Thunderjet cars stayed in the Aurora catalog in 1971 and 1972, but by 1973 all Aurora cars were AFX. In 1975 Magna-Traction cars appeared, and most of the earlier AFX cars were converted. AFX bodies snap onto the plastic chassis. Pickup shoes are spring loaded. Post-1972 cars have soft rubber rear tires. All but a few AFX car body patterns were either sculpted by Ron Klein or designed by staff artists Richard Ratkiewich, John Vernon, and Ken Hill for production by outside pattern shops.

1702 Grand Am funny car (1974), 87
1926 (MT)

blue/yellow/red	$100
white/red/medium blue	$25
yellow/orange	$30

Ratkiewich-designed body.

1703 Corvette "A" production (1974), 87
1927 (MT)

black/yellow	$60
bright yellow/black	$25

Ratkiewich-designed body.

1745 Datsun Baja pickup (1974), 87
1919 (MT)

blue/black #211	$25
mustard	$30
mustard #211	$25
lemon yellow/black	$30
lemon yellow/black #211	$20

Klein-sculpted body.

1746 1929 Model A Woody (1974), 87
1920 (MT)

black/mustard/brown "wood" side panels	$20

Different version of 1791, 1928. Vernon-designed body.

1747 Porsche 917-10K Can-Am (1974), 87
1921 (MT), 3001 (U5)

white/blue-red #16 (round front)	$20
white/blue-red #16 (square front)	$35
white/blue-red #23	$60

RC Cola logo stickers on nose and spoiler. RC Cola sold sets as premiums. Real car driven by Charlie Kemp in the 1972 Can-Am season. *Car Model* (November 1973) called it "the best model yet . . bar none!" Klein-sculpted body.

1748 Dodge Street Van (1974), 87
1922 (MT)

lime green/medium blue	$20
opaque green/medium blue	$30
yellow/orange	$20
orange/black	$20

"Specialty Chassis" like 1781 Roarin' Rolls. Ratkiewich-designed body.

1751 Ferrari Can-Am 612 (1971–74), 87
(RB)

bright blue #15	$20
bright orange #15	$20
red #15	$20
bright yellow/purple #15	$20
bright yellow/red #15	$20

Later issues of car came without wing. Klein-sculpted body.

1752 *Auto World* McLaren XLR (1971–74), 87, 88
(RB)

bright blue #54	$35
bright blue/black #54	$30
bright orange/black #54	$30
bright orange/dark blue #7	$65
bright orange/gray #54	$25
bright yellow #54	$30

Cars come with and without wing. Klein-sculpted body.

1753 Dodge Daytona Charger (1971–74), 91
1900 (MT)

bright blue/black #7	$35
orange/black #7	$40

red/black #7 $200
bright yellow/black #7 $30
lemon yellow/black #7 $30

Klein-sculpted body.

1754 "Too Much" (1971–74), 91
5788, 5812 (SC)

lime green/blue green $25
lime green/green & gold metallic $25
lime green/green & silver metallic $25
bright orange/purple $20
red/black $25
lemon yellow/black $20
lemon yellow/orange $20

Larger scale version used in Powerslicks 2151. HMS-designed body.

1755 "Turbo Turnon" (1971–74), 91
5787, 5811 (SC)

bright orange/purple/yellow chrome $20
white/red/blue stars $20
yellow/blue $20
lemon yellow/blue $20

Larger scale version used in Powerslicks 2152. HMS-designed body.

1756 Trans-Am Camaro Z-28 (1971–74), 91
1901 (MT)

light blue/purple #3 $30
white/medium blue #3 $25
white/orange #3 $85

Klein-sculpted body.

1757 Porsche 917 (1971–74), 91
1902 (MT), 1798 (AFT), 1973 (AFT)

light blue/orange #2 $25
white/purple #2 $20
bright yellow/medium blue #2 $15

Gulf Oil decoration (orange and light blue). Based on the car that won the 1970 World Grand Prix Championship. Teamed with Ferrari 512M (1763) in Grand Prix sets. Klein-sculpted body.

1758 1971 Plymouth 'Cuda funny car (1971–74), 91
5784, 5790 (SC)

blue/white $70
bright orange/yellow/purple $45
white/blue/red stripes $35
white/mustard/orange stripes $30
white/mustard/red $30
white/orange $30
white/red $30
white/red/medium blue $40
white/red/yellow $30
white/yellow/orange $40

Keeler wanted a line of funny car dragsters and asked Ratkiewich to design this, the first in the series. Rides on a regular chassis, but because of long body front wheels attach to body.

1759 1971 Vega Van "Gasser" (1971–74), 91
5781, 5782, 5783 (SC)

mustard/red flames $25
bright orange/red flames $25
white/fluorescent red-orange flames $55
white/red flames $25
bright yellow/red flames $25

Ratkiewich-designed body.

1760 1957 Chevy Nomad (1971–74), 91
1903 (MT)

medium blue $30
translucent blue $35
medium blue/silver stripes $80
brown $85
lime green $70
lime green/dark green stripes $70
lime green/silver stripes $90
bright orange $30
bright orange/light orange stripes $80
pink $55
pink/cranberry stripe $100
bright orange/blue exhausts $55
bright orange/white exhausts $55
lemon yellow/orange exhausts $55

Ratkiewich wanted a 1955, but Keeler chose 1957 because he remembered that a decade earlier the '57 Chevy he selected for Revell to make a model of became that company's best selling model kit. Ratkiewich-designed body. Classic design and wild colors made it one of Aurora's best-selling cars. Issued first in lime green.

1761 Pinto funny car (1972–74), 93
5785, 5789 (SC)

lime green/medium blue/silver $45
lime green/green/silver $25
translucent green/green/silver $25
bright orange/purple/silver $25
white/blue/silver $25

Ratkiewich-designed body.

1762 Plymouth Road Runner stock car (1972–74), 93
1904 (MT)

bright blue/red #43 $40
medium blue/white #43 $75
red #43 $100
red/blue #43 $70
red/white #43 $100
white/blue #43 $25
yellow #43 $55
yellow/orange #43 $20

Number 43 is Richard Petty's car, although Aurora didn't explicitly market the car as such. An unlicensed product during a time when few bothered with license agreements. Ratkiewich-designed body.

1763 Ferrari 512 M (1972–74), 93
1799 (AFT), 1905 (MT), 1974 (AFT)

ultramarine blue/yellow #6 $30
red/white/silver #2 $25
white/silver $25

Teamed with Porsche 917 (1757) in Grand Prix sets. Klein-sculpted body.

1764 Javelin Trans-Am (1972–74), 93
1906 (MT)

blue/black black #5	$25
blue/black silver #5	$20
mustard/black/red black #5	$25
mustard/black/red silver #5	$25
red/white #5	$30
red/white/ultramarine blue #6	$30

Mark Donahue won the Trans-Am series in the red/white/ ultramarine blue version of this car. Sears sponsored the AMC race team; Aurora built this car to please one of its largest customers, Sears. Ratkiewich-designed body.

1765 Javelin pro stocker (1972–74), 93

lime green/black	$65
orange/black	$50
white/purple	$110
bright yellow/black	$40

Same body as 1764 with air scoop on hood.

1766 Corvette funny car (1972–74), 93, 111
5786 (SC)

bright orange/purple	$40
white/red/medium blue	$35
bright yellow/black	$35

Ratkiewich-designed body. Rides on a regular chassis, but because of length of body front wheels attach to body.

1767 Lola T-260 Can-Am (1972–74), 92
1907 (MT), 3008 (U5)

white/red/black #1	$15

L & M logo stickers. Klein-sculpted body.

1768 Shadow Can-Am (1972–74), 92
1908 (MT), 3007 (U5)

black #101	$15

Shadow logo on spoiler, UOP on fender. Model of car sponsored by Universal Oil Products and driven by Jackie Oliver in the 1971 Can-Am season. Klein-sculpted body.

1769 Ford "Baja Bronco" (1972–74), 92
1909 (MT)

medium blue/black/white/chrome #3	$35
mustard/black/white/chrome #3	$60
red/black/white/chrome #3	$25
yellow/black/white/chrome #3	$25
translucent yellow/black/white/chrome #3	$25

Ratkiewich-designed and Klein-sculpted body.

1773 Dodge Charger stock car (1972–74), 92
1910 (MT)

lime green/black blue #11	$45
lime green/black red #11	$45
white/black red #11	$25
mustard/black red #11	$20

Ratkiewich-designed body.

1775 Bre-Datsun 240Z (1973–74), 92
1911 (MT)

red/white #46	$20

Initially available at Datsun dealers with special decals. Klein drove a real one and sculpted the HO body.

1776 Bre-Datsun 510 Trans-Am (1973–74), 92
1912 (MT)

blue/white #35	$25
red/white #35	$20
red/white #46	$25
turquoise/white #35	$40

Available initially at Datsun dealers with special decals. Aurora received permission from the Sports Car Club of America to use the "Trans-Am" race series trademark. Klein-sculpted body. Aurora R&D team member Bernhard raced one of the real cars.

1777 1955 Chevy Bel Air (1973–74), 92
1913 (MT)

bright blue	$30
lime green	$45
orange	$30
red-orange	$30
bright yellow/white headers/red	$35

Tinted window and air scoop are one piece. Ratkiewich-designed body; he regretted chrome strip on sides had to be broken because of overscale front wheel well. The red-orange re-creates original Chevy color.

1778 VW "Baja Bug" (1973–74), 92
1914 (MT)

green/blue	$30
lime green/blue	$30
translucent green/blue	$30
orange/black	$25
red-orange/black	$30
red/black	$30
red/white	$25
white/black	$50
cream/black	$60
snow white/black	$50
bright yellow/black	$30
translucent yellow/black	$35

Klein-sculpted body.

1781 Roarin' Rolls "Golden Ghost" (1973–74), 94
1923 (MT)

black/white	$20
white/black	$25
bright yellow/black	$20
translucent yellow/black	$20

"Specialty Car" on a chassis 1D4" longer than regular AFX chassis, with a narrow rear end to accommodate wide slicks and smaller front wheels. Four-gear (vs. five) drive train. Body mounted to one post, unlike regular clip-on bodies. Gold chrome. Twin drag chutes. Winged ghost hood ornament. Ratkiewich-designed body.

1782 Peace Tank (1973–74), 94
1924 (MT)

olive green	$20
translucent green	$20

"Specialty Car" on same chassis as 1781 Roarin' Rolls. Model has Chrysler Hemi engine. Turret swivels. Push down canon barrel and driver head pops up. Knot in cannon barrel reflects anti-Vietnam sentiment within Aurora's R&D team. Guitar on hood, beer can on rear. Driver inspired by Aurora president Diker. Vernon-designed body.

1786 Porsche 510K Can-Am (1973–74), 94
1915 (MT), 3002 (U5)

blue/yellow/red white #6 SUNOCO	$35
blue/yellow/red white #7 SUNOCO	$35
red/yellow/white #4 SUNOCO	$35
red/yellow/white #6	$30
white/red/black #6	$25
white/red/black #6 L & M	$25

Porsche-Audi sticker on side. Available first at Sears Christmas 1972 with special sticker. Spoiler tilts. Klein-carved body.

1787 Matador stock car (1973–74), 94
1916 (MT)

red/white/ultramarine blue #16	$45
white/blue #2	$25
yellow/red #2	$35

Available first at Sears Christmas 1972. Modeled on Mark Donahue's car as sponsored by Sears, one of Aurora's best customers. Ratkiewich-designed body.

1791 '31 Model A Ford panel (1973–74), 94
1925 (MT)

bright blue/black	$35
lime green/black	$25
translucent green/black	$30
mustard/black	$25
orange/black	$55

"Specialty Car" on same chassis as 1781 Roarin' Rolls. Different version of 1746, 1928. Vernon-designed body.

AFX Flamethrowers

1798 Flamethrower Porsche 917 (1972–74), 94
1757 (AFX), 1902 (MT), 1973 (MTF)

light blue/orange #2	$25
white/purple	$20
yellow/blue	$15

1799 Flamethrower Ferrari 512 M (1972–74), 94
1763 (AFX), 1905(MT), 1974 (MTF)

ultramarine blue/yellow #6	$30
red/white/silver #6	$25

1973 Magna-Traction Flamethrower Porsche 917 (1975–77), 102
1902 (MT), 1757 (AFX), 1798 (AFT)

light blue/orange #2	$25
white/green #2	$20
bright yellow/blue #2	$15

1974 Magna-Traction Flamethrower Ferrari 512 M (1975–77), 102
1905 (MT), 1763 (AFX), 1799 (AFT)

bright blue/white/silver #2	$20
red/white/silver #6	$30
red/yellow #21	$160
white/blue/silver #2	$20

1975 Magna-Traction Flamethrower Chevelle stocker (1977), 102
1929 (MT)

orange/white/black #17	$35
white/orange/silver #17	$25
bright yellow/red/black #17	$20

1976 Magna-Traction Flamethrower Charger Daytona (1977), 102
1753 (AFX), 1900 (MT)

blue/black #7	$30
yellow/black #7	$30
opaque yellow/black #7	$30

Dragsters

Aurora used the "specialty" chassis to accommodate wide slicks and an extension to produce a dragster chassis. Six-gear drive train, not the usual five. They were first issued with AFX motors, later with Magna-Traction motors. Came in a domed package with decal sheet. Richard Ratkiewich and John Vernon designed the bodies.

1772 Dodge Fever (AFX) (1973–74), 98, 99
1961 (Magna-Traction) 75–76

white/fogged yellow	$50

Same body as 1792. Ratkiewich-designed body.

1774 Furious Fueler (AFX) (1973–74), 98
1962 (Magna-Traction) 75–76

white/fogged yellow	$50

Same body as 1794. Vernon-designed body.

1792 Aztec (AFX) (1973–74), 98
1963 (Magna-Traction) 75–76

red metallic	$65

Same body as 1772. Ratkiewich-designed body.

1794 Dyno-Mite (AFX) (1973–74), 98
1964 (Magna-Traction) 75–76

white/fogged blue	$55

Same body as 1774. Vernon-designed body.

AFX Magna-Traction

In 1975 the AFX chassis was modified to lower the motor magnets close to the metal power strips in Aurora track. Magnetic attraction would thus hold the cars to the track during operation. Magnets show through the chassis bottom. Most existing AFX car bodies were modified to fit the new chassis; all subsequent new cars featured Magna-Traction.

1900 Dodge Charger Daytona (1975–77)
1753 (AFX), 1976 (MTF)

blue/black #7	$35
greenish-blue/black #7	$35
orange/black #7	$40
yellow/black #7	$35
translucent yellow/black #7	$35

1901 Camaro Z-28 (1975–77)
1756 (AFX)

light blue/purple #3	$25
white/blue/red/silver #6	$25

1902 Porsche 917 (1975–77)
1757 (AFX), 1798 (AFT), 1973 (MTF)

light blue/orange #2	$25
white/green/yellow #2	$20
yellow/blue #2	$20

1903 1957 Chevy Nomad (1975–77)
1760 (AFX)

blue	$30
greenish-blue	$30
orange	$40
orange/yellow stripes	$80
pink	$55
pink/cranberry stripes	$100
red/white stripes	$85

1904 Plymouth Road Runner (1975–77)
1762 (AFX)

bright blue red #43	$45
medium blue white #43	$55
red white #43	$100
red blue #43	$50
white black #43	$115
white blue #43	$20
yellow white #43	$20
yellow orange #43	$20

1905 Ferrari 512 M (1975–77)
1763 (AFX), 1799 (AFT), 1974 (MTF)

blue/silver	$15
blue/white/silver #2	$15
blue/white/silver #6	$15
red/silver	$15
red/white/silver #2	$15
red/white/silver #6	$15
white/silver	$15
white/blue/silver #2	$15
white/blue/silver #6	$15

1906 Javelin AMX Trans-Am (1975–77)
1764 (AFX)

blue/black black #5	$30
blue/black silver #5	$20
mustard/black/red black #5	$40
mustard/black/red/silver #5	$30
red/white/blue #6	$35

1907 Lola T-260 Can-Am (1975–77)
1767 (AFX), 3008 (U5)

white/red/black #1 L & M	$20

1908 Shadow Can-Am (1975–77)
1768 (AFX), 3007 (U5)

black/white #101 Shadow	$15

1909 Ford "Baja Bronco" (1975–77)
1769 (AFX)

medium blue/black/white/chrome #3	$35
mustard/black/white/chrome #3	$60
red/black/white/chrome #3	$25
yellow/black/white/chrome #3	$20
translucent yellow/black/white/chrome #3	$25

1910 Dodge Charger stock car (1975–77)
1773 (AFX)

mustard/black #11	$25
orange/black #11	$40
white/black #11	$25
bright yellow/black #11	$20

1911 Bre-Datsun 240Z (1975–77)
1775 (AFX)

white/lime green #46	$20
white/red #46	$20

1912 Bre-Datsun 510 Trans-Am (1975–77)
1776 (AFX)

blue/white #35	$30
red/white #35	$25
yellow/orange #46	$20

1913 1955 Chevy Bel Air (1975–77)
1777 (AFX)

bright blue	$30
lime green	$50
red-orange	$30
bright yellow	$30

1914 "Baja Bug" VW (1975–77)
1778 (AFX)

green/blue	$30
lime green/blue	$30
orange/black	$30
red-orange/black	$30
red/black	$30
red/white	$30
white/black	$50
cream/black	$60
snow white/black	$50
yellow/black	$30
translucent yellow/black	$35

1915 Porsche 510K Can-Am (1975–77)
1786 (AFX), 3002 (U5)

blue/yellow/red white SUNOCO #6	$35
blue/yellow/red white SUNOCO #7	$35
orange/yellow/white SUNOCO #4	$40
red/yellow/white #6	$25
white/green SUNOCO #5	$55
white/red/black #6	$25
white/red/black #6 L & M	$25
white/red/black SUNOCO #6	$45
yellow/blue SUNOCO #2	$45

Porsche-Audi on side.

1916 AMC Matador stock car (1975)
1787 (AFX), 1938 (Police), 1939 (Taxi)

red/white/blue #16 $45
white/blue #2 $30
yellow/red #2 $35

1919 Datsun Baja pickup (1975–77)
1745 (AFX)

blue/black #211 $20
mustard/black #211 $20
lemon yellow/black #211 $20

1920 1929 Model A Woody (1975–77)
1746 (AFX)

black/wood $20

1921 Porsche 917-10 Can-Am (1975–77)
1747 (AFX), 3001 (U5)

white/blue/red #16 $15
white/blue/red #23 $60

RC Cola logo on nose and spoiler.

1922 Dodge Street Van (1975–77)
1748 (AFX)

lime green/blue $20
opaque green/blue $30
orange $15
orange/black $10
bright yellow/orange $22

1923 Roarin' Rolls "Golden Ghost" (1975–77)
1781 (AFX)

black/white $20
white/black $25
bright yellow/black $20
translucent yellow/black $30

1924 Peace Tank (1975–77)
1782 (AFX)

olive green $20
opaque green $20

1925 1931 Model A Ford panel (1975–77)
1791 (AFX)

lime green/black $25
opaque green/black $25
mustard/black $25
yellow/black $25

1926 Grand Am (1975–77)
1702 (AFX)

ultramarine blue/yellow/red $75
white/red/blue $25
yellow/orange $30

1927 Corvette (1975–77)
1703 (AFX)

black/yellow $50
medium blue/white $50
chrome/light blue $30
chrome/red $25
white/blue/red/no stripes #7 $40
white/blue/red/no stripes/silver lights, gas cap #7 $40
white/blue/red/silver stripes #7 $25
bright yellow/black $25

The #7 car was inspired by the American flag and issued for the 1976 Bicentennial. Ratkiewich-designed body.

1928 Model A 1930 Ford coupe (1975–77), 104

black/black $35
bright blue/black $35
greenish blue/black $30
bright yellow/black $25

"Specialty" chassis. Different version of 1746, 1791. Vernon-designed body.

1929 Chevelle stocker (1975–77), 104
1975 (MTF)

blue/lime green #17 $140
white/orange/silver #17 $30
bright yellow/red/black #17 $30

427 on hood. Ratkiewich-designed body.

1930 AMC Matador stock car (1975–77), 104
3005 (U5)

orange/black/red/silver #5, 425 on hood $30
white/blue/red/silver #5 $25

Mark Donahue won Riverside in this car. Aurora built AMC cars because favored customer Sears sponsored the real race cars. Hill-designed body.

1931 VW Thing (1975–77), 104
Canvas top version of 1936.

blue/white $15
yellow/black $15

Vernon- and Ratkiewich-designed, Klein-carved body.

1932 Mercury stocker (1976–77), 104
3006 (U5)

light blue/white/dark blue #31 $25
white/black/gold #31 $25

"429CI" on hood. Modeled on the Woods Brothers stock car. Hill-designed body.

1933 Porsche Carrera (1976–77), 104

orange/blue/black #3 $20
white/black/burgundy #3 $20

Modeled on one of the set of matched Porsches used in the International Race of Champions. Hill-designed body. Vernon described the body as a "fat guppy," which challenged Aurora designers to devise paint schemes to make it look thinner.

1934 Vega funny car (1976–77), 104, 105

orange/white/red $20
white/orange/blue/silver $30

Body created by an independent design shop in Philadelphia.

1935 Capri funny car (1976–77), 105

blue/black/white #13 $30
blue/black/white #13 no #13 on hood $35

orange/white/maroon #13 $30
orange/white/maroon #13 with no #13 on the hood $35
white/green/blue #21 $25

Hill-designed body. In reality, a rally car.

1936 VW Thing roadster (1976–77), 105
Open top version of 1931.
brown camouflage $30
green camouflage $25

R&D team member Bernhard explains the camouflage: "Boredom had struck the R&D department!"

1937 Dodge Van rescue vehicle (1976–77), 105
Ambulance version of 1922.
red/white/gold $20
white/orange/red $20

"Rescue" on sides. Hill-designed top.

1938 Matador police car (1977), 105
1916 (stock version), 1939 (taxi)
blue/white/black $30
white/black $50

1939 Matador taxi (1977), 105, 106
1916 (stock), 1938 (police)
light blue $30
white $25
yellow $20

1941 1956 Ford pickup (1977), 105
black/red & white flames $45
black/yellow & red flames $55
red/white & blue flames $45

1942 Custom Van (1977), 105
orange/red $20
orange/violet $20
white/blue $20

1943 Ford Street Van (1976), 105
white/blue $15
black $30
tan/brown $15

G-Plus

Late 1975 saw the introduction of a series of new cars with an in-line motor—a total departure for Aurora. The in-line armature and magnets are visible from the underside of the chassis. The earliest cars have Mabuchi motors, the rest feature Singapore-made Aurora motors. Bodies snap onto ears on chassis sides. All bodies were sculpted by Ron Klein.

1731 Lola T-330 (1976–77), 108
white/blue/orange/chrome #7 $35
white/blue/light blue/red/chrome #7 $30
yellow/red/chrome #7 $30

"Lola 7" on spoiler.

1732 Ferrari 312 PB (1976–77), 108
red/yellow/silver #2 $45
red/white/silver #2 $30

1733 McLaren F-1 (1976–77), 108
white/orange #11 $25
white/orange #11 without air scoop $50
white/red/black #11 $45

Texaco/Marlboro logos. The white/red version is the 1974 World Grand Prix Championship McLaren of Emerson Fittipaldi; white/orange is that of world champion James Hunt.

1734 Ferrari F-1 (1976–77), 108
red/white/black #6 $35

Goodyear logo. Paired with the McLaren F-1 (1733) in the Monaco Grand Prix race set (2108). Represents Niki Lauda's Ferrari 312T.

1735 Indy Special (1976–77), 108
black/red-orange/yellow/white #1 $20
white/red-orange-yellow #1 $40

Goodyear logo.

1736 Ferrari Daytona coupe (1976–77), 108
yellow/green/black #16 $25
yellow/lime green/black #16 $25

1737 Rallye Ford Escort (1977), 108
green/yellow/blue #28 $25

1738 Elf F 1 (1977–80), 108
blue/white #4 $40

XLerators and XLerators II

XLerators were the first slotless race cars. They appeared in 1973 with AFX motors and were first offered exclusively by Montgomery Ward. Improvements led to XLerators II with G-Plus, first marketed in 1976. When XLerators II replaced first issues, catalog numbers changed; new numbers are indicated after the slash. Since the bodies were old Thunderjets, they attach by screw posts front and rear.

2741 Ferrari GTO 250 (1973), 96
1368 (Thunderjet 500 version), 1493 (FT)
red/white #1 $50

2742 Ford GT (1973), 96
1374 (Thunderjet 500 version), 1395 (CC), 1417 (WO), 1472 (TO), 1494 (FT)
blue/black #2 $80

2741 Camaro (1974–75), 96
1388 (Thunderjet 500 version), 1418 (WO), 1480 (TO)
orange/white #1 $35
red/white #1 $35
white/blue #1 $35

2742/2788 Pontiac Firebird hardtop (1974–77), 96
1402 (Thunderjet 500 version), 1478 (TO)
blue/black-silver #2 $45

blue/red & yellow firebird/#2 $40
yellow/black-silver #2 $40

2743/2783 Ford "J" (1973–77), 96
1382 (Thunderjet 500 version), 1430 (FT)
bright orange/black/silver #3 $15
red/yellow/white #3 $20
yellow/black/silver #3 $20
translucent yellow/black/silver $25

2744/2748 Chaparral 2F (1973–77), 96
1410 (Thunderjet 500 version), 1476 (TO), 1491 (FT)
lime green/black/silver #4 $30
translucent green/black/silver #4 $30
mustard/black/silver #4 $30
orange/black/silver $30
white/blue #4 $25
white/lime green #4 $20

2746 Chevy pro-stock Vega (1974–75), 96
orange/black/red #3 $75
white/black/green #3 $85
Body original with Xlerators.

2747/2785 Chevy Baja Blazer (1974–76), 96
orange/blue/white #4 $25
white/blue/red #4 $45
white/blue/black #4 $30
white/black/red #4 $30
yellow/black/orange #4 $30
Body original with Xlerators.

2781/2786 Mercury Cougar hardtop (1975–77), 96
1389 (Thunderjet 500 version), 1419 (WO), 1479 (TO)
mustard/blue/white #3 $35
white/blue/red #3 $40
white/black/red #3 $50

2782/2787 Willys "Gasser" (1975–77), 96
1401 (Thunderjet 500 version), 1474 (TO)
red/black/yellow #4 $50
white/black/blue #4 $70
yellow/black/green #4 $35

Ultra 5

This Aurora slotless race set was introduced in 1977. Cars were designated "A" or "B" depending on which power rails they ran.

3001 Porsche 917-10 Can-Am "A" (1977)
1747 (AFX), 1921 (MT)
white/yellow-blue-green #11 $25
white/yellow-blue-green #11 AURORA $25

3002 Porsche 510K Can-Am "B" (1977)
1786 (AFX), 1915 (MT)
light blue/yellow/purple #6 $30
white/yellow/blue/red #6 AUTOWORLD $20

3005 Matador stocker "A" (1977)
1930 (MT)
white/yellow/red #1 $25

3006 Mercury stocker "B" (1977)
1932 (MT)
white/red/blue #2 $25

3007 Shadow Can-Am "A" (1977)
1768 (AFX), 1908 (MT)
black/orange-yellow-white #3 $25
white/red-orange-yellow #3 $15
white/red-orange-yellow #3 GOODYEAR $15

3008 Lola T260 Can-Am "B" (1977)
1767 (AFX), 1907 (MT)
white/blue-green-yellow #39 $15
white/blue-green-yellow #39 LOLA $15

Screechers

Screechers were first sold in 1976 as a preassembled, battery-powered slotless set for young children. In 1977 car catalog numbers were changed; new numbers follow the slash.

Screechers sets

5755 Firemen's Thrill Show (1977)
26" x 17" base $60–$100

5756 Interstate Chase (1977)
33" x 22" base $70–$100

5757 Spider-Man Meets the Fly (1977), 110
33" x 22" base $80–$110

5758 Drag City (1977)
41" x 30" base $70–$100

Screechers Cars

5781/5801 Smokies Magnum Wagon police car (1976–77)
1759 (AFX), 5782, 5783 (SC)
white/black $15
Star of the Interstate Chase set 5756.

5782/5802 Rapid Rescue (1976–77)
1759 (AFX), 5781, 5783 (SC)
yellow/red "Rescue 1" $15

5783/5803 Super Chief (1976–77)
1759 (AFX), 5781, 578 (SC)
white/red flames $15
Star of the Fireman's Thrill Show set 5755.

5784/5804 Flaming 'Cuda (1976–77)
1758 (AFX), 5790 (SC)
white/red & tan flames $20
white/flames on top & sides $35

5785/5805 Pinto Thunderbolt (1976–77)
1761 (AFX), 5789 (SC)
light blue/dark blue/white $15

5786/5806 "76" Supervette (1976–77)
1766 (AFX)
white/red/blue stars #76 $20
off-white/red/blue stars #76 $20
white/black stars $15
Bicentennial commemorative.

5787/5807 Terrible Turbo (1976–77)
1755 (AFX), 5811 (SC)
blue/red/white #7 $15

5788/5808 Double Trouble (1976–77)
1754 (AFX), 5812 (SC)
lime green/blue $15
yellow/orange #5 $15

5789/5809 Potent Pinto (1976–77)
1761 (AFX), 5785 (AFX)
orange/blue #22 $20

5790/5810 Super Cuda (1976–77)
1758 (AFX), 5784 (SC)
orange/yellow/red $15

5811 Spider Mobile (1977), 110
1755 (AFX), 5787 (SC)
blue/red/white web $30
Star of Spider-Man Meets the Fly set 5757.

5812 Fly Mobile (1977), 110
1754 (AFX), 5788 (SC)
green/black fly paint $20

Road Burners

This 1977-only set was marketed as a battery-powered toy race set for younger children. Track was regular AFX issue. Cars have AFX bodies with air foils removed. Chassis and motor are from the G-Plus line with weaker magnets. Perhaps as few as 5,000 sets sold.

2001 Ferrari 612 Can-Am
1751 (AFX)
orange $20
red $20

2002 *Auto World* McLaren XLR Can-Am
1752 (AFX)
orange $20
red $20

Cigarbox Cars

Cigarbox Cars went on the market in 1968 and were superseded by Speedline later that same year. Chassis is die-cast metal with Aurora logo, name of car, and catalog number imprinted on the bottom. Wheels are T-jet. All of the bodies are T-jet, except for the Formula I racers specially created for this series. It is not certain if all cars listed were actually issued.

Cars were molded in standard Thunderjet colors, plus some plated cars in gold, peach, and plum.
Mint cars in the box sell in the $20–$25 range; loose mint cars, $10–$15.

Speedline bodies fit on Thunderjet chassis; collectors must be certain a body represented as a Thunderjet body is genuine and not a Cigarbox body. To tell the difference, look for small variations in the height of the screw posts—compare the unknown body to a genuine T-jet. Cigarbox posts are shorter.

53 Ice Cream truck (1972)
Good Humor promotional item $60

6101 Stingray (1968)
1356 (Thunderjet 500 version), 6801 (SL)

6102 Ferrari Berlinetta
1368 (Thunderjet 500 version), 6802 (SL)

6103 Mako Shark
1380 (Thunderjet 500 version), 6803 (SL)

6104 Ford "J"
1382 (Thunderjet 500 version), 6804 (SL)

6105 Ford GT
1374 (Thunderjet 500 version), 6805 (SL)

6106 Lola GT
1378 (Thunderjet 500 version), 6806 (SL)

6107 Ford XL 500
1386 (Thunderjet 500 version), 6807 (SL)

6108 Toronado
1379 (Thunderjet 500 version)

6109 Riviera
1357 (Thunderjet 500 version), 6809 (SL)

6110 Thunderbird
1383 (Thunderjet 500 version), 6810 (SL)

6111 Dino Ferrari
1381 (Thunderjet 500 version), 6811 (SL)

6112 Porsche 904
1376 (Thunderjet 500 version), 6812 (SL)
This is actually a Porsche 906, and is correctly identified in the Thunderjet 500 series.

6113 Cobra
1375 (Thunderjet 500 version), 6813 (SL)

6114 Chaparral
1377 (Thunderjet 500 version)

6115 Camaro
1388 (Thunderjet 500 version), 6815 (SL)

6116 Cougar
1389 (Thunderjet 500 version), 6816 (SL)

6117 McLaren Elva
1397 (Thunderjet 500 version)

6118 Mustang convertible
1371 (Thunderjet 500 version), 6818 (SL)

6119 Dune Buggy

6120 Mangusta
1400 (Thunderjet 500 version), 6820 (SL)

6121 Lola Ford Formula I
Yanchus-sculpted body.

6122 Ferrari Formula I
Ron Kohn sculpted body.

6123 Cooper Maserati Formula I
Yanchus and Brand-sculpted body.

6124 Lotus Ford Formula I
Kohn and Yanchus-sculpted body.

6125 Honda Formula I
Kohn-sculpted body.

6126 BRM Formula I
Kohn-sculpted body.

6127 Jaguar XKE
1358 (Thunderjet version)

6128 1965 Ford Mustang hardtop
1372 (Thunderjet version)

6129 AC Cobra
1370 (Thunderjet version)

6130 Pontiac Firebird
1402 (Thunderjet version)

6131 Willys "Gasser"
1401 (Thunderjet version)

6132 Hot Rod
1366 (Thunderjet version)

6133 Cheetah
1403 (Thunderjet version)

Speedline

Speedline cars replaced Cigar Box in the fall of 1968 and sold through 1969. Bodies have brighter metallic paint. Chassis are still Cigarbox—they even say Cigarbox—but wheels are hard plastic. Some were reissued in 1973. Most 1973 reissues are unpainted plastic and lack clear windows. Paper sticker on 1973 issues says "Made in Singapore." Mint cars on blistercards sell in the $20–$30 range.

6801 Stingray
1356 (Thunderjet 500 version), 6101 (CB)

6802 Ferrari Berlinetta
1368 (Thunderjet 500 version), 6102 (CB)

6803 Mako Shark
1380 (Thunderjet 500 version), 6103 (CB)

6804 Ford J
1382 (Thunderjet 500 version), 6104 (CB)

6805 Ford GT
1374 (Thunderjet 500 version), 6105 (CB)

6806 Lola GT
1378 (Thunderjet 500 version), 6106 (CB)

6807 Ford XL 500
1386 (Thunderjet 500 version), 6107 (CB)

6809 Riviera
1357 (Thunderjet 500 version), 6109 (CB)

6810 Thunderbird
1383 (Thunderjet 500 version), 6110 (CB)

6811 Dino Ferrari
1381 (Thunderjet 500 version), 6111 (CB)

6812 Porsche 904
1376 (Thunderjet 500 version), 6112 (CB)
This is actually a Porsche 906.

6813 Cobra GT
1375 (Thunderjet 500 version), 6113 (CB)

6814 Chaparral
1377 (Thunderjet 500 version), 6114 (CB)

6815 Camaro
1388 (Thunderjet 500 version), 6115 (CB)

6816 Cougar
1389 (Thunderjet 500 version), 6116 (CB)

6818 Mustang convertible
1371 (Thunderjet 500 version), 6118 (CB)

6820 Mangusta
1400 (Thunderjet 500 version), 6120 (CB)

6827 XKE Jaguar
1358 (Thunderjet 500 version)

6828 Mustang hardtop
1372 (Thunderjet 500 version)

6829 AC Cobra
1370 (Thunderjet 500 version)

6830 Firebird
1402 (Thunderjet 500 version)

6831 Willys "Gasser"
1401 (Thunderjet 500 version)

6833 Cheetah
1403 (Thunderjet 500 version)

6853 Volkswagen
1404 (Thunderjet 500 version)

6821 Lola Ford Formula I

6822 Ferrari Formula I

6823 Cooper Maserati Formula I

6824 Lotus Ford Formula I

6825 Honda Formula I

6826 BRM Formula I

6854 Dodge Charger
1407 (Thunderjet version)

6855 Ford Torino
1408 (Thunderjet 500 version)

6856 Alfa Romeo
1409 (Thunderjet version)

Super Speedsters

A few of the Speedline cars reappeared in 1975. Cars were manufactured in the Orient and blistercarded in the United States. Chassis is Cigarbox. Most cars lack clear windows. A blistercarded set of three cars sells in the $30–40 range.

Pontiac Firebird
1402 (Thunderjet 500 version)

Willys "Gasser"
1401 (Thunderjet 500 version)

Lola GT
1378 (Thunderjet 500 version)
Molded with a hole in the center of the roof so the car would whistle as it sped down a track.

Ford J
1382 (Thunderjet 500 version)

Flashback

In 1969 Aurora sold a playset that involved sending two cars racing back and forth on a drag strip of orange track. Propulsion came from two squeeze bulbs that pushed the cars out of the grandstand, down the track, into a large rubber band in the pit station, and back up the track to the grandstand. The cars had extra-large wheels, and thus the wheel wells were cut out to an extra depth. Chassis is Cigarbox.

6103 Mako Shark
1380 (Thunderjet 500 version)
metallic orange/silver stripe $30

6108 Toronado
1379 (Thunderjet 500 version)
metallic purple/silver stripe $30

HO Structures

Aurora began manufacturing HO buildings for model railroad layouts in the late 1950s. When Model Motoring arrived, Aurora issued six injection-molded plastic kits for slot car raceways.

658 Service Station (1961–62), 23
$150
"Model Motoring Service Center." White/red/gray/clear plastic. Garage bay doors open. Decals for Texaco or Aurora signs. Designed to work with both HO model railroad and slot car layouts, the synergy did not work and the kit was discontinued after two years.

1450 Start-finish pylons (1963–73), 22
$20
White plastic. Spring-loaded flags flip up when hay bale is pressed.

1451 Judges stand (1963–73), 13, 22
$45
Gray plastic. Paper flag sheet included.

1452 Grandstand (1963–73), 22, 24
$45
Brown/gray plastic. Includes TV cameras and "Aurora Model Motoring Grandstand" decal.

1453 Double station pit stop (1963–73), 22, 25
$60
Beige/gray plastic. "Corvette" and "Thunderbird" sign decals.

1456 Curved bleachers (1963–73), 22
$35
Dark brown plastic. Decal sheet with real-life advertisements; paper pennant sheet. Curve fits the radius of Aurora's 9" curved track section.

1498 Start-finish pylons and judges stand (1974–77), 100
$35
Repackage of 1450, 1451.

1499 Grandstand, dual pit stop, curved bleachers (1974–77), 100
$70
Repackage of 1452, 1453, 1456.

Super Model Motoring

Issued at the height of the slot car boom, these 1/48 scale cars were intended to find a niche between HO cars and 1/32 scale. They are powered by regular T-jet motors. Hot rod-style bodies were all designed by HMS.

1751 1931 Ford Hot-Rod pickup (1964–65), 37, 38

gray/black	$100
red/black	$60
tan/black	$60
turquoise/black	$60
white/black	$60
yellow/black	$60

1752 1932 Ford chopped sedan (1964–65), 38

gray	$100
red	$60
tan	$60
turquoise	$60
white	$60
yellow	$60

1753 1936 Ford convertible coupe (1964–65), 38

gray	$100
red	$60
tan	$60
turquoise	$60
white	$60
yellow	$60

1754 1957 Chevrolet coupe (1964–65), 38

gray	$120
red	$80
tan	$80
turquoise	$120
white	$80
yellow	$80

1755 1949 Mercury Hot Rod coupe (1964–65), 38

gray	$100
red	$60
tan	$60
turquoise	$60
white	$60
yellow	$60

1756 1957 Thunderbird Hot Rod coupe (1964–65), 38

gray	$120
red	$125
tan	$80
turquoise	$80
white	$80
yellow	$80

1757 1927 Ford T Hot Rod (1964–65), 38

gray	$85
red/tan	$65
tan/brown	$65
white/green	$85
white/red	$60
yellow/brown	$60
yellow/green	$60

1758 1932 Ford Deuce Hot Rod (1964–65), 38

gray	$100
red	$75
tan	$65
turquoise	$65
white	$65
yellow	$65

Aurora 1/32 Cars

Between 1965 and 1967 Aurora issued ten cars in the Aurora Americans A-Jet series. The bodies were the same as Aurora's static model kits and K&B kits numbered 1825–1833. Unlike the K&B kits, Aurora's cars were ready-to-run. They had injection-molded bodies with chrome-plated and clear parts, A-Jet Sidewinder motors, aluminum frames, and rubber tires. Braided wire pickups were centered near the slot so cars would run on other track brands. Most had American flag stickers on their doors and wide racing stripes across their tops in a variety of colors, but some came without flags or stripes.

3251 Ford GT (1965–67), 46

white	$75

3252 Pontiac GTO coupe (1965–67), 46

red	$60-70
white	$60-70
yellow	$60-70

The GTO and Mustang were the most common bodies used in race sets.

3253 Mustang 350GT (1965–67), 46

red	$60–$70
white	$60–$70
yellow	$60–$70

The Mustang and GTO were the most common bodies used in race sets. Aurora's original static kit is a stock Mustang fastback; this slot car version became a Shelby 350GT with the addition of a hood scoop.

3254 Corvair Corsa coupe (1965–67), 46

yellow	$75

3255 Plymouth Barracuda (1965–67), 46

red	$75

3256 Chaparral (1965–67), 46

white	$75

3257 Cobra coupe (1965–67), 46

blue	$75

3258 Comet Exterminator (1965–67), 46

red	$75

3259 Lola T-70 (1966–67), 46, 47

blue	$80

Released a year after the initial eight cars.

3260 Rover BRM (1966–67)
dark metallic green $300
Extremely rare; it was released near the end of the A-Jet series.

The following four cars were listed in Aurora's 1966 and 1967 catalogs but apparently were never issued.

3261 Demolition Derby Buick
The prototype pattern was sculpted for this car.

3262 Demolition Derby Mercury
The prototype pattern was sculpted for this car.

3263 66 Oldsmobile Toronado

3264 Mako Shark
Aurora issued a static kit of this car.

3266 Thundercycle (1967), 53
red cycle/black rider $200
yellow cycle/black rider $200
Although sold to run on 1/32 track, the bike and rider are scaled at 1/24. Injection-molded body, chrome spoked wheels, Challenger motor, and aluminum frame. Two "training wheels" drive the cycle and keep it upright. Sold separately for $9.95 or in the Thundercycle Racing Set (3204). *In the Groove* (May 1967) noted that it ran more slowly than a car: "Wait till you check the handling. Good thing the poor guy is wearing leathers."

Big Car Racing

After a lapse of two years, Aurora revived 1/32 cars in 1970 with a home race set which included four cars and, in 1971, two tricycles. They have injection-molded bodies, plastic chassis, and in-line motor. Power pickups are metal shoes, and the power strips are positioned away from the slot. Clip-on braided pickups were included with each set so cars could be converted to run on conventional 1/32 track.

3351 Ferrari 612 (1970–71), 70
blue $70
red $70
Does not have real car's wing. Klein-sculpted body.

3352 McLaren M12 (1970–71), 70
orange $70
white $70
Does not have real car's wing. Klein-sculpted body.

3353 Mirage coupe (1970–71), 70
blue $80
orange $80
Klein-sculpted body.

3354 Ferrari 312P coupe (1970–71), 70
red $80
Klein-sculpted body.

3357 Green Machine (1971), 53
black/metallic green. $130
Three-wheel chopper cycle with "Crazy California styling." Designed to lift front wheel with acceleration. Sidewinder motor. Ratkiewich-designed body.

3358 Chopper Chariot (1971), 53
pink/purple $130
Three-wheel cycle. Ratkiewich-designed body.

Powerslicks

Powerslicks came from Aurora's toy division. Battery-powered to run on their own special track. Plastic chassis attaches to the front and rear. Powerslicks have wide plastic front tires and rubber rear tires.

2151 Two-Much (1970–71)
black/metallic gold $30
black/metallic red $30
AFX version of this car body is 1754. HMS-created body.

2152 Turbo-Turnon (1970–71)
black/metallic green/metallic gold $30
AFX version of this car body is 1755. HMS-created body.

2153 Mod Rod (1970–71)
black/metallic gold/metallic red $50
Dodge Challenger; Innova-created body.

2154 Drag'n Devil (1970–71)
blue/red/white $50
Opel GT; Innova-created body.

2155 Bad Bandito (1970–71)
black/metallic copper/black $50
black/metallic purple/silver $50
Mustang; Innova-created body.

2156 Wild Winger (1970–71)
black/metallic blue/white/silver $50
Ferrari; Innova-created body.

K&B 1/32 kits

Aurora subsidiary K&B's boxed kits contain a blistercard with the injection-molded plastic car body, chrome-plated parts, clear plastic windows, Challenger Sidewinder motor, adjustable aluminum frame, aluminum wheels, rubber tires, and decal sheet with a selection of race numbers and stripes. They sold for $6. Bodies are from Aurora static kits and were also used for Aurora Americans A-Jets nos. 3251–3259. These 1/32 kits are harder to find today than K&B's larger scale kits.

1825 64 Ford GT coupe (1965–67), 46
white $200
GT-40.

1826 65 Pontiac GTO coupe (1965–67), 46
dark blue $200

1827 65 Mustang GT-350 (1965–67), 46
white, blue paint trim $200

1828 65 Corvair Corsa coupe (1965–67), 46
light yellow $200

1829 65 Plymouth Barracuda (1965–67), 46
dark red $200

1830 64 Cobra Daytona coupe (1965–67), 46
blue $200

1831 64 Chaparral 2 (1965–67), 46
white $200

1832 65 Comet Exterminator coupe (1965–67), 46
red $200

1833 65 Ford Lola T-70 (1966–67), 46, 47
blue $200
Car Model (September 1967): "K&B's Lola T-70 is more of a caricature than an accurate model of the real Lola's lines."

K&B INJECTION-MOLDED 1/32 CAR BODIES

Kits contained the same injection-molded plastic bodies, with clear and chrome plated plastic parts and a decal sheet. They sold for $1. Today they sell in the $50 range.

1825-1 64 Ford GT coupe
white $50
A GT-40.

1826-1 65 Pontiac GTO coupe
blue $50

1827-1 65 Mustang GT-350
white $50

1828-1 Corvair Corsa coupe
light yellow $50

1829-1 65 Plymouth Barracuda
red $50

1830-1 64 Cobra coupe
blue $50

1831-1 64 Chaparral 2
white $50

1832-1 65 Comet Exterminator
red $50

1833-1 65 Ford Lola T-70
blue $50

K&B 1/32 CLEAR CAR BODIES

Clear bodies were vacuum-formed from butyrate plastic. They were blistercarded on a "Model Rama Pit Stop" card with a decal sheet and sold for 89 cents. Typical collector's price: $7-10.

1321 32 Ford coupe (1964–67)

1322 32 Ford two-door sedan (1964–67)

1323 Ferrari GT (1964–67)

1324 Porsche RSK (1964–67)

1325 Porsche GT (1964–67)

1326 Lister Corvette (1964–67)

1327 Jaguar XKE (1964–67)

1328 Corvette Sting Ray (1964–67)

1329 BRM (1964–67)

1330 Indy Car (1964–67)

1331 Southern California Sportsman (1964–65)

1332 Cooper F-1 (1964–67)

K&B 1/25 SCALE CAR KITS

308 Dragmaster 64 $300
Aluminum frame and wheels, spring-loaded pick up arm, "German Slick" tires, decals. More a frame than a car, though it does have a driver's head. No motor—drag enthusiasts would buy or make their own. Originally $6.95.

1800 64 Ford GT coupe (1965)
white $160
A GT-40 LeMans racer. Body based on the prototype. Also issued by Aurora as a model kit. Wheels attach to threaded axle. $7. Reissued as 1811.

The 1800 and 1801 kits were K&B's first large scale kits and the only ones issued in 1/25 scale. Clear windows molded into the injection-molded body. Decals. Challenger aluminum chassis and wheels with chrome plastic spoked-wheel inserts. Tires stamped "Goodyear." Challenger motor. Originally sold for $8.

1801 Shelby Cobra Daytona GT (1965)
medium blue-gray $165
Model Car & Track (April 1965) criticized the shape of windows and headlights but praised the car's performance. Wheels attach to threaded axle. $7. Reissued as 1812. The Japanese company Otaki copied this car, making a few changes in details and molding it in red-orange plastic.

K&B 1/24 CHALLENGER CAR KITS

These kits followed the 1/25 kits but contained new features: Posi-Lok wheel attachments, and most received improved 6-volt Super Challenger motors.

1802 65 Porsche 906/916 (1965), 48, 49
silver gray $130

Porsche supplied K&B with design data. Issued with Challenger motor before Super Challenger was available. Box art by Jack Leynnwood. $7. Reissued as 1813.

1803 Ferrari 250 GTO/64 (1965), 48, 49

maroon $140

Model Car & Track (June 1966) notes model is based on Ferrari belonging to English sports car buff George Drummond, down to tag number "M09-1553." Issued with Challenger motor before Super Challenger was available. $7. Reissued as 1814.

1804 65 Sebring Chaparral (1966–67), 48

white $160

#66 decal. Super Challenger motor. Posi-Lok wheels. $8.

1805 65 Lola T-70 (1966–67), 47, 48

metallic blue $160

Miniature Auto (May 1966) praised the body as a "real work of art," but noted it wasn't accurate. Also noted decals don't match the real car, especially the "Firestone" decal for a car which ran on Goodyear tires. Super Challenger motor. Posi-Lok wheels. $8.

1806 330 P2 Ferrari (1966–67), 48

metallic maroon $250

Super Challenger motor. Posi-Lok wheels. $8.

1811 Ford GT (1966–67)

white $160

Reissue of 1800 in a new white box showing car's profile. Motor upgraded to Super Challenger and wheels attach with Posi-Lok. $8.

1812 Ford Cobra coupe (1966–67)

light metallic blue $400

Reissue of 1801 in a new white box with new art showing only the profile of the car. Lighter metalflake blue replaces earlier blue plastic. Old box art is on box insert. Body mold retooled to add glue-on rear spoiler, rivets and two air scoops on the hood, and brake vents on the sides; changes reflect modifications made by Ford to the original Cobra prototype and incorporated into the car that raced LeMans in 1964 and 1965. Motor upgraded to Super Challenger and wheels attach with Posi-Lok. $7.95.

1813 Porsche 906/916 (1966–67)

silvery gray $270

Reissue of 1802 in a new white box showing car's profile. Old box art is on box insert. Motor upgraded to Super Challenger. Posi-Lok wheels. $7.95.

1814 Ferrari 250 GTO/64 (1966–67)

maroon $200

Reissue of 1803 in a new white box showing car's profile. Old box art is on box insert. Motor upgraded to Super Challenger. Posi-Lok wheels. $7.95.

K&B 1/24 Ready to Run Cars

1850 64 Ford Lotus 30 Charger (1965–67)

orange $115

green $115

Plastic body shell; no metal chassis. Royal Bobcat motor mounted as sidewinder. Posi-Lok wheels. Jose Rodriguez, Jr., of *Car Model* noted body detailing was poor and attributed it to cost cutting. $9.95. Rugged construction made this a popular rental car at commercial slot raceways.

1851 Cooper F-1 Wildcat (1966–67)

white $115

Plastic body shell; no metal chassis. Wildcat 9-volt motor. Posi-Lok wheels. $8.95.

1852 The Sportsman (1966–67)

dark red $150

Clear vacuformed body painted inside. One-piece aluminum chassis, fall away pickup. Royal Bobcat motor mounted as sidewinder. Posi-Lok wheels. Model of a quarter-mile super-modified stocker. $10.95.

1853 65 Mako Shark (1966–67)

blue metalflake body $150

Vacuformed body. Kangaroo chassis. Hellcat motor mounted as sidewinder. Cortina Brake. $13.95 Superkit.

1854 McLaren Mark 2 (1966–67)

white $150

Vacuformed body. Nonadjustable metal chassis, Super Challenger motor. "K&B" decal. Based on no. 97 car of Charlie Hayes, sponsored by K&B. $6.95.

1876 Chaparral 2D (1967)

white $150

Vacuformed body. Kangaroo chassis. Jaguar motor. Hells Bells sponge tires. $10.95.

1876 Alfa Romeo Canguro

Announced in 1967, but never issued. Planned features: injection-molded body, Hellcat motor mounted as sidewinder, priced $8. With Cortina brake as Superkit, $13.95.

1877 65 Ford GTX-1 roadster

Announced in 1967, but never issued. Planned features: injection-molded body, Hellcat motor mounted as sidewinder, priced at $8. With Cortina brake as Superkit, $13.95.

1878 Batmobile (1966)

black $600

Vacuum-formed body, injection-molded windshield, chrome-plated parts, red body stripes, Hellcat motor mounted as sidewinder, Cortina brake, blinking red Batlight, $14.95. K&B made this car after Aurora 1/32 static model became a runaway bestseller. K&B President John Brodbeck noted the slot car "laid an egg" because it was a poor racer. K&B had a license for the Green Hornet's Black Beauty, but never issued the car.

1879 Ford-Cobra Bordinat

Announced in 1967, but never issued. Planned features: injection-molded body, Hellcat motor, Cortina brake, $13.95.

1895 Blue Monster (1966–67)

blue/yellow $500

Vacuum-formed body painted metallic blue, yellow stripes. McLaren I car body. One-piece aluminum chassis. K&B ran a 1966 "Blue Monster Bonanza" contest in race centers to publicize introduction of the new Blue Monster motor. Advertised as superfast, reviewers in slot magazines rated it good, not outstanding. $12.95.

Jupiter
Announced in 1967, but never issued. $13.95

Ford GT Mark II (1967)
blue, fogged silver paint $250
Hot Shot Inline chassis. Inline 26-D Jaguar motor. Cortina brake. $12. Final K&B slot car.

K&B injection-molded 1/25 and 1/24 bodies

Kits had the same injection-molded bodies as in the motorized kits above, with clear and chrome parts and decal sheet. $1.29.

1800-1 Ford GT coupe 1/25
white $45

1801-1 Ford Cobra coupe 1/25
Medium blue-gray $90

1802-1 Porsche 906/916
silver gray $45

1803-1 Ferrari GTO/LM
maroon $45

1804-1 Chaparral 2
white $50

1805-1 Ford Lola T-70, 47
blue $50

1806-1 Ferrari 330 P2
metallic maroon $80

1850-1 Lotus 30
orange $45
green $45

K&B 1/25 scale clear bodies

Bodies were vacuum-formed from clear butyrate plastic. Sold for 98 cents. Today collectors pay around $10.

1301 Corvette Sting Ray
split window

1302 Jaguar XKE

1303 32 Ford coupe

1304 59 Corvette hardtop

1305 32 Ford Victoria

1306 Maserati Tipo 61 Birdcage sport coupe

1353 McLaren Mk II
$200
Comes in a nice clear case; inside body painted white. #97 decal, blue & red stripe. Niki Chevrolet.

1360 Batmobile
$100

Motors

Although hard to find, all the motors listed below can be purchased in the $10–$25 range.

1500 K&B Royal Bobcat 36D Mabuchi, 55
9-volt, yellow can, white endbell

1501 K&B Bobcat 36D Mabuchi, 55
12-volt, yellow can, white endbell

1502 K&B Challenger Aurora-built sidewinder, 55
12-volt, bare metal and black or white plastic

1503/1504 K&B Super Challenger Aurora-built side-winder, 55
6-volt, bare metal and black plastic. Major visible difference between a Super Challenger and Challenger is the cylinder containing the commutator—added to the side of the Super Challenger.

1505 K&B Wildcat 16D Mabuchi, 55
9-volt, yellow can, white endbell

1506 K&B Cougar 13D Mabuchi, 55
9-volt, yellow can, white endbell

1508 K&B Jaguar 26D Mabuchi
3-volt, chrome can, white endbell

K&B Blue Monster 36D Aurora-built
6-volt, black endplates, motor held together with blue metal clips. The version of the Hellcat (1510) used in the K&B Blue Monster (1895) and not sold separately.

1510 K&B Hellcat 36D Aurora-built, 55
12-volt, black endplates, motor held together with black metal clips. K&B version of Aurora Blue Monster.

1553 K&B Challenger Aurora-built sidewinder, 55
12-volt, bare metal and black or white plastic. Stock motor of early K&B kits; same as the K&B 1502 and Aurora 3250 A-Jet.

3250 Aurora A-Jet Aurora-built sidewinder
12-volt, bare metal and black or white plastic. Stock motor of early Aurora A-Jet cars; same as the K&B Challenger 1502 and 1553.